PRAISE FOR
WORK THAT'S WORTH IT

"Georgi Enthoven has a compelling idea—you have about 90,000 hours in your working life, and the key to your well-being is to use those hours to do good. Rather than chasing money, tune in to your heart. I've been privileged to mostly be able to do this in my life and can attest to how well it works. Having a purpose that aligns with Mother Nature gives me a reason to get up early and savor each day."

—**CRAIG FOSTER,** filmmaker, *My Octopus Teacher*; founder, Sea Change Project

"The ability to uplift others—the essence of true leadership—is built on a foundation of self-understanding and purpose. Georgi Enthoven's *Work That's Worth It* is a crucial starting point for young professionals seeking to build this foundation. By guiding readers to leverage their careers as a force for good, Enthoven is nurturing the authentic, impactful leaders our world needs."

—**FRANCES FREI,** professor, Harvard Business School

"Every individual possesses a unique essence that makes them an original. *Work That's Worth It* illuminates the importance of unveiling that singularity and sharing it with the world as part of life's mission."

—**ALONZO KING,** founder and artistic director, LINES Ballet

"What we are born with is only one half of the puzzle. What we do with what we have makes the difference and expands the world. *Work that Worth It* illustrates how no one is too small to achieve success or make that difference, and the world is waiting for your contribution!"

—**JUDY WILKINS-SMITH,** author, executive coach, and trainer

"Meaningful progress on long-standing social issues will depend on the fresh ideas, energy, and work of the next generation. *Work That's Worth It* provides emerging leaders with the inspiration and permission to dream, balanced with the tools to translate those dreams into a rewarding and impactful career."

—**AMELIA ANGELLA,** director, Social Enterprise
Initiative, Harvard Business School

"Through *Work That's Worth It*, Georgi Enthoven has masterfully crafted a proven road map that demonstrates how to create both impact and income, weaving together inspiring stories of those who are already living it. By spearheading this transformative initiative, Georgi is equipping the leaders of today and tomorrow with the tools to achieve true fulfillment. The force for good behind this movement isn't just inspiring—it's destined to move mountains and change lives."

—**MATT LEBRIS,** host, *Decoding Success* podcast

"*Work That's Worth It* challenged me to reconsider my professional connections. I'm now driven to collaborate with brands that align with my values. This book and community will empower you to transform how you spend your time and impact in the workplace."

—**KIRA AKERMANN,** founder and
entrepreneur, METRIC Research

"*Work That's Worth It* is a must-read guide for young professionals seeking to deepen their career impact and self-awareness. As a realist, I found Georgi's idealistic yet grounded approach encouraging. She provides clear and practical pathways to understanding one's professional place and purpose."

—**JENNA-LEA KELLAND,** freelance
copywriter and editor

"Georgi Enthoven's book, *Work That's Worth It*, is the book that every college graduate should read before embarking on their career."

—**JACK CANFIELD,** best-selling author
and cofounder, Chicken Soup for the Soul

"*Work That's Worth It* is the ultimate guide for young professionals and students ready to build careers that matter—without sacrificing their financial stability or burning out. Teaching graduate students, I see firsthand how today's generation wants work that feels meaningful, makes a difference, and still pays the bills. Georgi Enthoven nails it with a mix of practical tools, real talk, and inspiring stories that show you how to align your strengths, values, and goals. This book is your go-to playbook for creating a career you love—one that works for you, the world, and your well-being."

—KATE ATTEA, senior lecturer and associate director,
Social Sector Leadership program, University of Chicago

"Georgi Enthoven has created a transformative guide for anyone seeking to fill their 90,000 work hours with purpose, impact, and meaning. As someone who has dedicated my career to helping individuals and organizations align their passions with meaningful work, I am deeply inspired by her mission to redefine success. As a new mother, her message resonates even more profoundly, reminding me of the importance of aligning our professional lives with what truly matters—for ourselves, for the planet, and for future generations.

Georgi's work is a call to action for anyone ready to align their career with their values, and I know it will inspire countless individuals to pursue meaningful, impactful work that truly matters."

—STEPH JACK, founder, Ethical Earth Studios;
branding expert; and conservationist

"As someone who recently entered the workforce, Georgi Enthoven's *Work That's Worth It* was everything I didn't know I needed. Its impactful honesty and inspiring guidance are exactly what every young person my age needs to be reading post-college graduation. With empathy and leadership, Georgi guides you to realize that your career is more than just a paycheck; it is a path to personal and universal fulfillment."

—EMMA MAYER, publicist, Gracie PR;
graduate student, George Mason University

"What a missed opportunity for me not to have this book twenty years ago. Like several examples in the book, I looked at work as a binary: either work for financial rewards and some professional satisfaction or sacrifice fair compensation and make a difference. There were no models for being a 'Well-Rewarded Disruptor.' Thanks to this insightful and practical book, *Work That's Worth It*, young people can now tap into their most authentic selves and become the future leaders we sorely need."

—**DIANE JONES LOWREY,** social impact leader; head of
diversity, equity, and inclusion, Common Sense Media

"Finally, a career guide that speaks to the real challenges and opportunities facing purpose-driven professionals today! As a brand strategist working with changemakers, I see firsthand how many talented people feel trapped between meaningful work and financial stability. Georgi Enthoven's *Work That's Worth It* provides both the inspiration and practical tools to break free from this false choice. Her concept of the 'Well-Rewarded Disruptor' isn't just theoretical—it's a road map for the future of work we desperately need."

—**LARISSA SALAZAR,** personal brand strategist,
Brand Builders Group

"Leading Kardias, a nonprofit dedicated to saving children's lives in Mexico, has shown me the profound joy of finding fulfillment in my work. I was inspired and gained clarity by understanding my own capacities, which allowed me to align my purpose with meaningful action. Georgi Enthoven's book *Work That's Worth It* offers a practical framework to help others do the same—discover not just a job, but a true calling that brings both personal satisfaction and a lasting impact."

—**LOLA FERNANDEZ,** general director, Kardias

W♥RK THAT'S WORTH IT

THE AMBITIOUS PROFESSIONAL'S GUIDE FOR A HIGH-IMPACT, HIGH-REWARD CAREER

GEORGI ENTHOVEN

RIVER GROVE
BOOKS

Published by River Grove Books
Austin, TX
www.rivergrovebooks.com

Distributed by River Grove Books

Design and composition by Greenleaf Book Group and Sheila Parr
Cover design by Greenleaf Book Group and Sheila Parr
Cover image used under license from Adobe Stock: 326069086/M-KOS
Graphics by Michele Bell

Grateful acknowledgment is made to the following for permission to reproduce copyrighted material.

The New Yorker Cartoon Bank: For "Cartoon "I don't think reusable straws are going to be enough" by Sarah Kempa from *The New Yorker* Collection. Reproduced by permission of *The New Yorker* Collection Cartoon Bank. All rights reserved.

Publisher's Cataloging-in-Publication data is available.

Print ISBN: 978-1-63299-943-6

eBook ISBN: 978-1-63299-944-3

Hardcover ISBN: 978-1-63299-957-3

First Edition

*To all those with big hearts and curious minds
who yearn to be part of something
meaningful and greater than themselves.*

*And to my three children,
may this book expose you to
exciting and fulfilling pathways
that I never knew existed,
inspiring you to shape a better world.*

CONTENTS

THE POWER OF YOUR 90,000-HOUR CAREER

IS A FULFILLING CAREER TOO idealistic? Perhaps you're tired of hearing people tell you that "the world needs you!" It adds to the pressure you already feel about creating a successful career. Adding "a positive impact" into the mix: Can you really solve real problems in the world *and* experience personal growth and financial stability at the same time?

Just like so many young professionals experience today, when I was getting started with my career, I remember struggling to choose between doing something good for the world and earning the salary I wanted. I ideally wanted to pursue both, but I lacked ideas, role models, and examples of how to combine impact and income. It always seemed to be one or the other.

Motivated students on college campuses are still being recruited under this outdated choice, even though they are craving something realistic that aligns more closely with their values and ambitions. Of course, on the extremes, there are students who view their career as either a commitment to altruism, or alternatively, a 100% focus on accumulating wealth without a second thought for anything else. However, most young professionals today fall somewhere in the middle and are grappling with this artificially limiting choice, and the compromises weigh on them heavily.

If you're one of those in the middle, perhaps you will relate to one or more of the following statements that represent this push/pull on your values as you negotiate the tension between income and impact:

- You are deeply motivated by the contribution you are making in the world yet struggling with the sacrifice of your personal income. You notice that you're resenting your peers who can afford to go on vacation and get their first mortgage.

- You work in sustainability for a large corporation where you are gaining valuable skills. However, the company itself is a significant contributor to the global plastic pollution problem. You wonder if your impactful work is making a big enough dent to make it worthwhile, or if it's just a greenwashing publicity tactic.

- Post-college you are focused on being a worthy investment for your parents knowing what they sacrificed on your behalf, and therefore have decided to build a financially driven career. However, you can feel the lack of alignment, and you wonder when you will have the freedom to lean into *your* dreams. In the meantime, you compensate for your choices by volunteering at charitable organizations outside of work.

- While you are on the fast track to financial success, you generously donate up to 10% of your income to causes that appeal to you. You've convinced yourself that effective altruism is the best way for you to positively impact your community. But something still feels not quite right, especially the mindset of your coworkers.

- Your day-to-day job looks impressive, but you're unsure if this is the right career ladder for you to climb in the long term. Unfortunately, you don't have time to stop and reconsider. Is this really what you will be doing for the next 40 years? Is this all you'll accomplish in your career?

Your parents likely faced these dilemmas early on in their careers too, and you probably witnessed the struggles and consequences of their choices from the sidelines. Perhaps you're already experiencing signs that sacrificing personal dreams at the altar of your chosen cause or ambition comes at a cost. Although it may take time to notice, regret, resentment, burnout, and feelings of purposelessness are common in those who feel they could have used their careers more wisely. However, as yours progresses, it also becomes harder to change direction, which can lock in your misalignment until retirement. But do you really want to wait for your second act to make a difference in the world? It doesn't have to be that way.

Making It Worth Your Time

You can build a career that enables you to make meaningful differences without sacrificing personal sustainability. In fact, the most exciting career opportunities are the ones that combine both income and impact. Together, we'll discuss methods, stories, and exercises that will empower you as a young professional to build a long-lasting, rewarding career that benefits both you and the world.

Luckily, in the last few decades, the concept of business as a force for good has birthed many valid and admirable businesses around the globe, along with new role models for shoulders to stand upon. They are paving the way for a more diverse and exciting professional highway. These businesses offer proof that today, your career can be fulfilling, motivating, and well-compensated—meeting the needs of the most ambitious workers.

There is a sweet spot where you can minimize the compromises and discover a harmony of your strengths and passions working in tandem for long-term impact. It requires some introspection, expansive thinking, and intentional choices. As a result, you build a strong foundation for your career and become a Disruptor for Good in the world.

Finding the right industry sectors and roles may take extra diligence, creativity, and persistence, as they're less deeply entrenched than traditional banking or technology positions. The stories I'll share will expose you to examples and role models already on this path. In addition, there are introspective exercises to prepare for success ahead.

For-profit businesses are increasingly noting their role in addressing urgent global challenges, in tandem with government, nonprofits, or nongovernmental organizations (NGOs). Many large industry sectors recognize their potential for solving important problems in the world and benefit humanity or the planet with innovative business models. Sadly, it's not happening fast enough, but pressure is mounting—which in turn is building momentum in the right direction. Well-known companies like Microsoft, Apple, Procter & Gamble, and Walmart are committing to reducing their carbon footprints, setting ambitious goals for 2030 and 2040. Larger institutions are tracking and reporting their ethical and sustainable practices using indicators for reporting ethical, sustainable, and corporate governance issues. Clean energy sectors are booming, with significant demand for new electricians and green jobs. Technological advancements in various fields, such as transportation, agriculture, education, and healthcare, are working toward contributing to a more sustainable future. Circular business models and local, ethical production practices are gaining traction, promoting recycling, and reducing waste.

Workers are also asking more from their employers than ever before. Many young employees value purpose alongside their paychecks. Reportedly, 75% of people in the US are either "not engaged or are actively disengaged at work," including those with college degrees. According to a 2022 LinkedIn survey, 87% of Gen Z professionals would consider changing jobs for a company that aligns more with their values, and 94% of Gen Z consumers believe companies should address environmental and social issues.[1]

Opportunities in companies aligned with ethical values and environmental sustainability are increasing, offering competitive salaries. Progressive companies are designing their financial models around the impact they envision from the get-go, allowing workers to earn fulfilling salaries while achieving high impact. Emerging success metrics like the Green Domestic Product (GrDP), which factors in the depletion of natural, social, and human capital; the Genuine Progress Indicator, which includes factors such as distribution of wealth and impact on the environment; and the Happy Planet Index, which focuses on achieving long, happy, and sustainable lives are all challenging how we measure and value economic growth and reflect evolved values.[2] There are now more than 9,000 B-Corp–certified companies globally that are held to higher but worthy standards.[3] However, greenwashing and misinformation are still challenges. Employers are using buzzwords like "sustainability" and "social impact" to attract young workers, but Gen Y and Z are paying attention and see through these superficial efforts, which adds to the pressure to change for the better.

This younger generation of workers are vocal and use social media to pressure companies to align with their values and do as they say. They want to understand a company's mission before accepting a job. These purpose-driven workers will use their influence for the greater good as they rise to leadership positions down the road. This shift is exciting for both the planet and business.

Aligning Your Career with Your True Self

According to *Harvard Business Review*, the average person's career amounts to 90,000 hours.[4] That's an enormous amount of time—a third of your adult life. What if you could use those 90,000 hours for something positive—a career that harnesses your talent and ambition? One that is *worth it* for you and also helps the world we live in?

You can turn your 90,000 hours into a force for good by building a solid foundation for your career. To feel aligned, it is crucial that you first understand yourself well. To do that, you will need to know your genuine interests, strengths, skills, values, and talents and must develop the ability to communicate your talents to attract the right opportunities. You must establish your personal mission and determine where you want to contribute to the world. You'll have to determine what is most important to you to engage in a career that fulfills you on many levels. It is crucial that you know how you want to be rewarded or compensated for your hard work and also that you build your community to advance your efforts. You'll need to learn the importance of working through problems, becoming comfortable with conflict and growth, and you'll also need to understand what you need in the work world and the burgeoning markets that are set to make essential changes in problems worth solving. Finally, you must think expansively about what drives you, so that you can experience a flow state while engaged with your work.

Putting in the self-discovery work early in your career sets you up for a lifetime of alignment and clarity to move forward with confidence. The evidence is in the lives of those I've coached over the past five years, as well as the testimonies and inspiring stories of the world-changing and hardworking people I share in the chapters ahead. Through these examples, you'll understand how to combine both a meaningful contribution and compensation to match in your career, avoiding having to juggle values or zigzag between the two different ideals. By prioritizing your personal sustainability, you enhance the capacity and resilience to continue making meaningful contributions for an exciting career over many years.

Your career is about more than just earning a paycheck. How you use your time shapes and defines who you are as a person, who you spend time with, your life experiences, and what you leave as a legacy.

Your work molds you, so ask yourself, "Who do I want to be?"

This approach leads to the most exciting and challenging opportunities out there. It also ensures that your fulfillment from your job extends to enriching rewards and compensation that are not just monetary. Instead of waiting until you hit a breaking point or missing your calling completely and living a life of regret, I encourage young professionals to discover early on how to make a career beneficial for both themselves and the world. By making your work worth your time, you can succeed in that dream.

> Your work molds you, so ask yourself, "Who do I want to be?"

Worth It for Me

I noticed a comic in *The New Yorker* by Sarah Kempa a few years back. In it, two friends sip drinks on a sofa while watching the news. A map on the TV showed heatwave after heatwave. The tagline was, "I don't think reusable straws are going to be enough."

"I don't think reusable straws are going to be enough."
Credit: Sarah Kempa / The New Yorker Collection / The Cartoon Bank

While using humor to touch on global warming, the comic sparked a strong desire in me to contribute to something more than giving up a few conveniences, such as straws. While billions can adopt planet-friendly habits, changing entrenched systems and conveniences is an overwhelming challenge. It requires momentum, willingness, and likely a disruptive force for good.

And it requires large corporations and businesses to claim their responsibility, too.

As a mother of three wonderful kids, I'm genuinely concerned about the state of our planet and the future we're leaving to our children (and grandchildren). Truthfully, I feel ashamed of the choices we humans have made in the name of unsustainable growth and our negative impact on our planet.

Instead of solely relying on consumers to change their behavior (such as giving up straws), what if we raised the bar for our 90,000 career hours (innovating beyond plastic straws altogether)? That gave me hope and inspiration to contribute my part. My family of five alone could contribute 450,000 hours. My Harvard Business School class theoretically could contribute upward of 72 million hours. That feels like a powerful sum of hours and is very motivating.

As I dug into my research, conversed with workers and employers, and career-coached young professionals, it became clear that impactful work was not as simple as a line with "harmful" to the left and "helpful" to the right. Workers needed to meet their own personal needs too, which led me to focus on solutions that benefit the world without sacrificing your own needs. So that's what I'm on a mission to do—help you realize and seize the good choices out there so you can contribute in a way that's beneficial for you and for the world! This journey began with a cartoon about straws and grew into a vision of aligning professionals and companies to make responsible and rewarding decisions for our collective future.

Who Determines Your Impact?

Through conversations I've had, many people ask, "Who determines your impact?" My answer: you do! You determine what's important to you.

When you understand what you're capable of, where you can contribute, and how you can multiply it, you can then determine how to best use those tools for the positive outcome you want to see. Maybe you're already part of solving an important problem in the world, or perhaps you're unsure how to follow avenues of social change without putting aside corporate ambitions and desires for financial stability.

Do you want to embrace the privilege and opportunity to make a difference? With the right tools and questions, you too can gain a sense of accomplishment in your career while receiving valuable compensation for your time, skills, and efforts. The choice is yours.

Our World Is Waiting for Your Talents

"The most important right we have is the right to be responsible," said Gerald Amos, an indigenous Haida leader from Canada, according to Vincent Stanley, the outdoor clothing manufacturer Patagonia's first employee. Stanley elaborated: "The right to be responsible gives us a sense of agency. If you see responsibility as a burden, you lose that sense of choice and freedom, making it onerous. But if you turn it around and think, 'I have the right to be responsible. I have the right to act on behalf of what I care for and love,' it becomes empowering."[5]

What if you embraced your right to be responsible—not as a duty, but as an exciting opportunity? As captured by the cartoon about the straws, adverse world events ignite an urgency to make social and environmental changes for ourselves and our planet. Safeguarding the Earth and the health and happiness of humanity is available to everyone motivated to contribute.

How will you build a career that's *worth it*? Ready to figure it out? Let's get started!

Throughout this book, you'll find a collection of stories and experiences that highlight the concepts in each chapter. While these stories are captured at a specific moment in time, their essence and the lessons they impart are time-less. The individuals and organizations mentioned continue to evolve, yet the core principles remain constant. They are here to show you what's possible when you commit to using your professional life as a vehicle for positive change.

CHAPTER 1

THE WELL-REWARDED DISRUPTOR

I HAVE A CLIENT—LET'S CALL her Grace—who fits a common profile of many young professionals doing good things in the world: *the unrewarded do-gooder*. Grace is an example of the kind of person we need to nurture and encourage as a business leader. She's driven and talented, and she wants to positively contribute to something greater than herself. However, she also represents all potential do-gooders who offer their time and energy in service of others without paying sufficient attention to their own needs.

Grace currently lives in Seattle and works full-time for a well-established international foundation. She holds a BA from a top US university known for technology and innovation, and even though she has yet to become an American citizen (she holds a green card), she has been able to create a strong network of like-minded, ambitious colleagues and feels at home in her adopted country.

Like many young adults, Grace's academic success in college turned into various summer internships, and then she made it through a highly selective process to land her first job shortly after graduation. She understood how to achieve in the system laid out in front of her, and although she was successful in entering her initial career path, she never gave the bigger picture of her career trajectory much thought.

In her current job, Grace is focused on making healthcare more accessible in emerging markets, although she is conscious that the people who benefit from her contribution are often thousands of miles away. Her work requires significant travel and she often spends two weeks a month working from their Central Africa office and visiting local rural health clinics. This in-person action is hugely important. It's allowed her to gain deep knowledge of the last-mile supply chain in her region, and she has been fortunate to have personal conversations with the real people benefiting from her work. Without this understanding and connection, she would not be as effective at her job.

Her empathy toward others is one of her most resounding strengths. She can see or sense in a room what others might miss completely. This attribute has not always been recognized as an asset by her or others, so she sometimes masks it by being highly organized and well-prepared, coming across as a competent high achiever and less "emotional." However, she's also learning that it makes her exceptional at times, allowing her to connect people and ideas long before others can see the possibilities.

Ultimately, because of her sensitivity, she is also more prone to leaning into this empathy and her compassion beyond what is sustainable; she's at risk of burnout unless she tends to her own needs. What perpetuates this is that she feels such a large sense of responsibility—being an only child, firstborn to an immigrant family—and she hates to let anybody down or disappoint the people she cares about. To appear strong, she has a pattern of not asking for help.

Grace is acutely aware of how different her life choices are from those of her grandparents, who were subsistence farmers in Latin America. Her diverse background brings her tremendous compassion and connection to people living very different lives from hers, and she is always curious about others and how they live. In her role, she is a valuable bridge connecting the financial resources from the US to the medical needs of a different continent. She is ambitious and dedicated to contributing positively to the world, motivated by the impact she has on the people she helps.

Grace is now approaching her thirtieth birthday and is reflecting on what's next for her. She has a strong work ethic and a sense of purpose. The company she works for is considered best-of-class in what they do, and she has been very successful both in the organization and in her area of impact. People in her network always tell her they admire her so much for the work she does, and she has enjoyed several promotions already and an impressive title too. That all feels good. But she came to me feeling discouraged, dissatisfied, and unsure of her next move.

She is noticing that her successful peers from college are starting to consider buying apartments and treating themselves to vacations. And as she looks ahead at the leaders in her company, that's not the case for them (other than those pooling financial resources with a partner or significant other). She knows she wants to have a positive impact in the world, but she is also feeling conflicted for the first time. Her annual income is $65,000 for her impactful role, which, in Seattle, means saving very little—if anything—even though she has two roommates and keeps her bills to a minimum. Her parents live in a different country and are aging. They will need her financial support not too far down the road, and she's an only child. So she really feels this looming responsibility of taking care of her parents, making the idea of potentially starting her own family daunting.

Although she cares deeply about the work that she's doing day to day, her contribution is just scratching the surface of what's actually needed in her current region, and she wonders if she is making a meaningful dent. Surprisingly, she feels envious of the less-weighty jobs of her peers and of the financial freedoms they are beginning to enjoy. She feels conflicted and doesn't like this side of herself, but it's there.

Grace feels stuck—she's at a crossroads in her career. She feels less motivated each time she has to jump on a plane to cross multiple time zones, landing on the other side of the world in every sense. She wonders if she's experiencing some depression, or perhaps she's merely burnt out. Either way, her mental health is suffering and she doesn't know how to balance her desire for more income with her desire for a positive contribution to the world.

Grace is confused about what boundaries to draw for her personal well-being. She knows that she needs to make a change. But what are her options? Would investing in a graduate school program later grant her more financial freedom? Or perhaps switching to the for-profit sector? Should she join an investment bank or venture capital firm to maximize her earnings while she's young and can work long hours, returning to meaningful work later in her career?

She worries that any of these options could require her to abandon the important work she was drawn to, which she still believes is valuable. She's aware that her next job will need to allow her to begin saving. Although Grace is looking for answers, she lacks role models to guide her through this stage in her career.

What she wants and needs is guidance about the options that are available to her.

The stress Grace feels from wanting a higher salary from her job is a double-edged sword. She is limited financially and feels concerned about not having saved for her future. Then there's the feeling of guilt for even wanting more, given that she makes ends meet and has such a "great" job that offers her the chance to help people in need. Why isn't that enough for her?

There's good news for Grace. There is lots of time for her to transition from an "unrewarded do-gooder" to what I call a "well-rewarded disruptor." Let me explain.

To feel aligned and contribute positively to our world through our long careers, we have traditionally been faced with a limited either-or choice: we either make an impact or we prosper financially. How can we expect ambitious and motivated adults who are looking for fulfilling work to settle for less income, an inability to support their own families, and a limited ability to influence key decisions? New business models and incentives are constantly emerging that offer people like Grace beneficial work *plus* the possibility to prosper individually. To be sure, 90,000 hours is a long time, and to avoid burnout, more awareness of your individual needs is essential. When your impactful work is personally rewarding, the benefits multiply beyond the hours you put in.

Contribution Plus Compensation

As someone who is giving a large amount of her attention and energy to doing really important work in the world, Grace is starting to show predictable signs of burnout. She needs help exploring what she is *receiving* in return for all those hard hours. Grace is only one archetype of this imbalance: the Unrewarded Do-Gooder.

She has strived to contribute to the betterment of the world—to have an impact, as she defines it—while foregoing sufficient rewards for herself, her family, and her future. This perceived low level of reward feels like she is sacrificing her own needs for others, and she's ready to give up. She finds it exhausting and deflating, and she finds herself thinking about what else she could have done with her career hours, which decreases her motivation.

Let's revisit the crossroads. At its corners, we have four extremes that show how positively contributing to the world and being compensated well for your work can be represented in our professional lives (see Figure 1.1). We all find ourselves in one of these boxes at times, and we likely touch different ones during the various stages of our career journey.

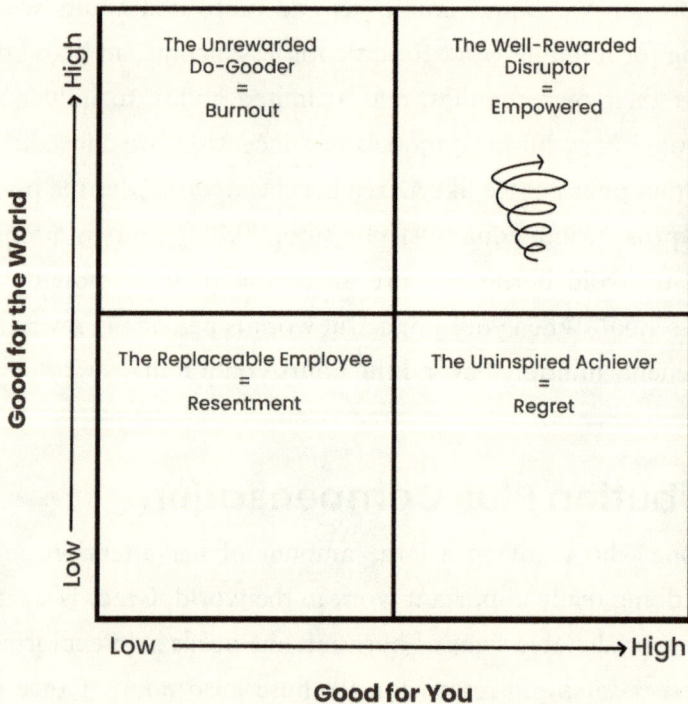

High	The Unrewarded Do-Gooder = Burnout	The Well-Rewarded Disruptor = Empowered
Low	The Replaceable Employee = Resentment	The Uninspired Achiever = Regret

Good for the World

Low ————————————————→ High

Good for You

Figure 1.1. The Four Extremes of Doing (or Not Doing)
Good for Yourself and for the World

Across the diagram from Grace's Unrewarded Do-Gooder is the Uninspired Achiever. This person is ambitious and highly compensated financially but ignores their desire to connect with some deeper inspiration for their work hours. They might gain some satisfaction from their financial situation, but they often feel empty and purposeless, although that may not surface for a while. This feeling can be overwhelming. It can lead to regret later in life when they realize how hard they worked, how much joy they missed out on, and how little they contributed to something greater than themselves. They don't feel proud of their work and may even feel embarrassed about how they made their money. This can lead to emptiness and regret, and people in this category sometimes look for a second career where they can "make up" for their perceived lack of a wider contribution earlier in their career. But most often, the switching cost later in their career becomes too great, or they run out of time.

At the nadir of these factors, many employees feel both the lack of any larger contribution and a lack of compensation, which is not good for them and contributes nothing to the world. This position often leads to resentment, frustration, and unhappiness over many repetitive years. It's the prototypical hourly wage worker, the Replaceable Employee. They don't feel connected to the company they work for beyond the paycheck and benefits they receive. There is also a limited likelihood of promotion or upward mobility. They are not asked to bring creativity and ingenuity to their work; instead, they are asked to perform predictable tasks within formulaic guidelines. They feel bored by the tasks required, have little personal interest, and experience exhaustion. Their jobs are easy to quit, and they are—or at least are made to feel—easily replaceable. They are underwhelmed with their career and their impact, and they can, understandably, lack motivation. Their jobs are not likely aligned with their values. It's just a paycheck and a means to an end. They leave it all at work after hours, and they feel disheartened, underestimated, and uninspired.

Back to the Well-Rewarded Disruptor. The opposite of the resentful hourly worker bee is empowerment. When you feel you're making a meaningful contribution to society or the betterment of humanity, the environment—whatever your cause is—and you are also compensated at a level that fills your cup, you have everything you need to tap into your highest potential. You become a Well-Rewarded Disruptor—specifically, a disruptor for good. Not only are you proud of the work you do, but you're also energized to keep going for the long haul. And most often, the direct benefits of your good work in this quadrant indirectly spill over to further your impact in other areas—essentially multiplying your efforts, which is even more rewarding.

These four identities are based on the perception of the employee. Two people with the exact same role at a company can perceive themselves as being in different quadrants. For example, one teacher may feel sufficiently rewarded for her role, while another may not. This is because we don't share the same values and priorities. You alone can determine your current placement.

The world can't afford to lose Grace to the Uninspired Achiever quadrant, which is a real possibility as she feels pressure to plan for a future for herself and her family. Accepting that we as humans have caused significant damage to our planet, nurturing the kind-hearted among us is essential—and urgent. To remain committed to doing valuable work in the world, more businesses and leaders must find—or create—employment opportunities that appropriately reward the efforts of the people doing that important work. Luckily for the world, Grace cares about contributing to something meaningful. She also feels pressure to make that contribution not just from within herself but also from her teachers, her peers, and perhaps all of humanity. She can feel both the intrinsic and extrinsic pressures loud and clear, and she is curious to explore solutions that match her evolving desires more closely. There are so many opportunities in the world to solve important problems we're facing. Whether it's local or international, our planet's problems won't get solved without driven people like Grace: those who are naturally wired to contribute to something greater than themselves. Although Grace is still finding her footing, there are pathways for her that allow her to do great work and be rewarded for it, moving her to the Well-Rewarded Disruptor quadrant, where she can tap into her full potential *and* feel empowered.

Becoming and remaining a Well-Rewarded Disruptor works best when you take the time to consider your career on multiple dimensions, mindfully reflecting on your possibilities. This is craftwork, requiring practice and intentionality; we could call it *job craft* or, even better, *career craft*. To craft your career, you, like Grace, will need to find a path that is beneficial for the world, as well as being rewarding for you personally.

CHAPTER 2

THE UPWARD SPIRAL FOR GOOD

WHAT WOULD YOUR CAREER LOOK like if you solved a real problem in the world and had the security and satisfaction of a well-compensated job? Although most people still think they are faced with an either-or decision of impact or income, I want to demonstrate where there can be overlap between these so-called choices. With this awareness you can begin noticing more options that feel aligned and inspiring—for you and for the world.

I'm sure you have witnessed a pattern like this in some form already: you engage in work that is beneficial to our world, tapping into the generosity of your heart. As it takes its form it creates a domino effect, inspiring others to follow suit. When they are aligned, both the giver and the receiver benefit personally from this state, encouraging a continuous cycle—a win-win effect that compounds and spirals upward toward even better things. This spiral allows you to attract opportunities effortlessly. And it represents you at your best, in a flourishing state. I call this the Upward Spiral for Good that occurs when you are contributing positively to the world, plus fulfilling your own dreams.

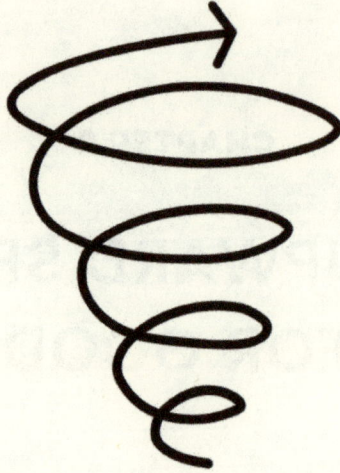

Figure 2.1. The Upward Spiral for Good

Getting to Know a Disruptor for Good

Sami Inkinen is an extraordinary entrepreneur who is a remarkable example of the Well-Rewarded Disruptor and someone who has created this positive spiral through his work. He is the Finland-born cofounder and chief executive of Virta Health, a US-based health-care company founded in 2014. Their bold mission is to reverse diabetes and obesity in 1 billion people without requiring medications or surgery.[1]

I'm sure we all know someone with diabetes. In the US alone, over 11% of the adult population have type 2 diabetes—almost 40 million Americans.[2] And over 96 million US adults have prediabetes. It's estimated that diabetes costs the US $237 billion yearly in direct medical costs and $90 billion in lost productivity.[3] And these upward trends are not unique to the US.

Sami got interested in diabetes for personal reasons, which is often how we find a calling that deeply motivates us. Although he is an extreme athlete, competing in triathlons, and has broken the world record for rowing from San Francisco to Hawaii, his bloodwork surprisingly indicated that he was prediabetic. In his thirties he was fit and seemed healthy. He perceived himself to be a health icon, and instead of accepting an eventual diabetes diagnosis, he started researching how he could reverse the trajectory to becoming a diabetic. Through his research he learned that the American diet, heavy on carbohydrates and processed food, was not favorable for many reasons. Specifically, it directly contributes to the diabetes epidemic we see around the world. Through diet experimentation, Sami tried eating a keto-based diet, reaching ketosis. By changing his diet alone, his health recovery went through an impressive turnaround that inspired him to build the company Virta Health.

Previously, Sami cofounded the highly lucrative leading online real estate company Trulia. In 2012, the company went public on the New York Stock Exchange and later merged with Zillow in 2014. He left at this time ready to leverage his entrepreneurial skills and cocreated Virta Health. To date, he has raised over $360 million and Virta is valued at $2 billion.

Already a successful entrepreneur, Sami was aware of his unique strengths, skills, and values before starting Virta. For example, one of his most notable strengths is that he likes a big challenge. Because of this, he set the bar high for Virta. "If you're trying to do something transformative, and 50% of people you talk to are like, 'Oh, yeah, that's cool. I think that's possible,' the bar you've set is not high enough," he says. "To get real transformation, 95% of people have to think you're crazy."

Contributing to something larger than himself was automatic for Sami. Initially, he was motivated to solve his health concerns, but even more exciting than serving his own needs was to apply that knowledge to help others. "My massive transformative purpose was reversing diabetes and obesity in 1 billion people. . . . We're not there yet. But there's no stopping now."

He also has a high-risk tolerance—a helpful trait for any entrepreneur. He believes that playing it safe is not the way to get things done. He wasn't born into wealth to grant him that golden parachute; it's in his DNA. "When you are starting out and have no mortgage, no spouse, and no kids, your risk tolerance is the greatest it will ever be. If everything goes sideways, so what? It's such a tiny risk. So do your thing, start your thing. Whatever you want to do, start early to truly follow your excitement and craziness."

And as you may gather, the fear of failing is not a barrier for Sami either. "If you're afraid of failing, which, I think, is the number one reason people play safe, know this: nobody cares [if you fail]. But what if you go for it and succeed? Well, maybe they still won't care. But at least you'll get a lot of accolades and help a lot of people. Stop worrying about others."

For Virta to have the greatest impact on diabetes and obesity, Sami and his founding team deliberately decided to set it up as a for-profit business. "It wasn't because I need to personally make as much money as I can, but because it's the best vehicle to deliver on my goal," he says. Although he considered all his options, he decided that a not-for-profit would limit his success: "I'd forever be begging for money from donors. It was very clear to me that if you have a world-changing idea and want to make it scalable to millions of people, you can get the capital to ultimately build a machine that keeps funding and feeding itself. And it attracts the best talent, unlike many not-for-profits." He was clear about what he wanted to offer the world, and he aligned Virta's business decisions to set his team up for success.

Sami and his team designed the business model by noticing how each stakeholder would benefit from reducing diabetes and obesity in his future patients. Today, although you can sign up as an individual for their program, most of their customers are offered the service as a benefit through their employer. Those employers benefit when their employees become healthier, are more productive, and need less time off work. And it's cheaper to pay Virta Health than to cover the increased insurance premiums of a patient diagnosed with diabetes, so that's also a win for the employer. It's a model designed to help everyone. It's better for the patient with diabetes and offers a secondary benefit for the caretakers in their families. It's more economical for the employer. And it is beneficial financially and emotionally for the corporate Virta employees who feel satisfied that their work contributes positively to the world, including for Sami. This is the Upward Spiral in action.

Sami's success in life has not come from him alone. People are behind his story in all ways. His success has required hardworking values-driven parents with Finland ethics, caring teachers, classmates, colleagues, friends, a spouse and kids, partners, investors, cheerleaders, coworkers, and loyal customers—some of which have even tattooed the Virta logo on their bodies! "The number one thing that I would advise before you get out in the world is to slow down a little to focus on building really deep relationships with other people wherever possible," says Sami. "I try not to regret anything in life. But when I was still at university doing my master's in physics, I did not invest as much time as I should have building relationships. I had two jobs. I was just super busy. In retrospect,

I think students should work less and just spend time with your student friends and others everywhere you go."

As an already financially successful entrepreneur, money alone didn't motivate Sami to create Virta. "My career advice to [my]self and to others contemplating starting (or joining) a company is to always ask two questions: 'Do I understand the true purpose of the company I'm starting or joining?' And 'Does that purpose resonate at some deeper level than just making a buck or only providing momentary excitement?' If the answer is an obvious Yes, the magic can happen."[4]

Sami says plainly: "Why do something just to make money and then use 10% of those proceeds to do good? Why don't you allocate 100% of your time to do good with your daily work? Society, particularly capitalistic America, is creating this illusion that money is going to make you happy. Trust me, it's going to do nothing. There is no gold at the end of the rainbow. Don't chase the gold at the end of the rainbow. Chase the rainbow and enjoy the walk [along the way].

"You're helping people with every single one of the minutes and hours that you spend." The challenge to reverse diabetes and obesity at scale makes up a large portion of the reward Sami requires at this stage in his life, but the for-profit status ensures that his employees of Virta receive both satisfaction and a competitive wage, which draws more people to his cause.

So far, a great deal of good has happened for a lot of people thanks to Virta Health. Their patients were able to reduce their A1c marker for diabetes by an average of 1.3% (plus reducing the need for diabetes medications).[5] Over a two-year period, 97% of people in the Virta peer-reviewed trial did not progress to type 2 diabetes, with many reversing their condition entirely.[6] Furthermore, Virta's patients were able to lose an average of 12% body weight by the one-year mark.[7]

Will Virta reach its ambitious goals? Maybe yes, maybe no. Regardless, the real value, according to Sami, is doing something worthwhile. "When you do something meaningful," he says, "it's inspiring. Nobody's inspired by 'Yeah, we're trying to help three people to improve their diabetes.' Setting a big goal is inspiring—inspiring for investors, for team members, for journalists and the press. It's very helpful, very motivating for others and yourself as well. And if this works out, wow, this was definitely worth it."

Sami has leveraged his entrepreneurial spirit, skills, and network to build a company that creates enormous benefits in many people's lives. Virta is reversing a negative spiral of a poor diet that often leads to prediabetes, which progresses to diabetes and eventually results in premature death. Sami built a company that is disrupting for good. He is well rewarded for his efforts in ways that are meaningful to him too. It's a positive cycle for good—an "upward spiral."

No Degree Needed

Sami's story is iconic in many ways, but you don't need an advanced education or deep expertise to be a Disruptor for Good. A great recent and important example of the Upward Spiral for Good in action is Greta Thunberg, the Swedish environmental activist. It started with her kind and generous heart perceiving the urgency to make better decisions for our planet, so she decided to take action. In 2018, at the age of 15, Thunberg started skipping school on Fridays to protest outside the Swedish Parliament, demanding stronger action on climate change. Her solo protest soon gained attention and inspired other students around the world to join her in what became known as the Fridays for Future movement. Students in cities across the globe began organizing school strikes and climate protests, calling on governments to take urgent action to address climate change. Through her advocacy, Greta leaned into her unique combination of capabilities, including her courage, effectively conveying her message with clarity and conviction. She demonstrated resilience to the unnecessary backlash of people threatened by her impressive abilities to rally a crowd as she continuously advocated for the fragile living world around her. She has already received numerous awards and honors, including being named *Time* magazine's Person of the Year in 2019. She has also been nominated for the Nobel Peace Prize multiple times. More than that, she has created space for neurodiverse people to follow in her footsteps, and to make noise to fight for change.[8]

Sailing the 7 Cs

Creating a career that's *worth it* starts with a mindset shift: the desire to work in a way that feels aligned with something larger than yourself. When you experience work in the Well-Rewarded Disruptor quadrant, where you and the world benefit from your work hours, you almost always experience the Upward Spiral. I work to help people build careers where they can make a meaningful contribution and be compensated for their impactful work so that the Upward Spiral of giving and receiving keeps going—and becomes exponential.

Instead of leaving it to chance, there are some essential building blocks that will increase your likelihood of achieving this spiral. They are also likely to get you there faster and with more clarity. If you're a young professional, the pressure to land a prestigious job can motivate your choices before you have even had a chance to explore who you are, what you value, and what you are interested in. In fact, in many elite colleges in the US, a career path to banking and management consulting starts freshman year through selective clubs. But once you've entered your first job, most people go about their careers jumping from one opportunity to the next every few years. They do not have a clear idea of where they are ultimately navigating toward beyond their next move. Although frequent promotions, corporate perks, and an impressive career title are good for the ego (and your student debt), the cumulation of short-term choices can lead to long-term misalignment and dissatisfaction in our careers. Most people don't invest the time to direct their careers with a long-term view. More often professionals consider only one or two steps ahead, to the next job title or promotion in sight.

> If you're a young professional, the pressure to land a prestigious job can motivate your choices before you have even had a chance to explore who you are, what you value, and what you are interested in.

Being mindful of these 7 Cs will allow you to be intentional with your career; where your head, heart, and body agree; and how your most satisfying and valuable work can be realized.

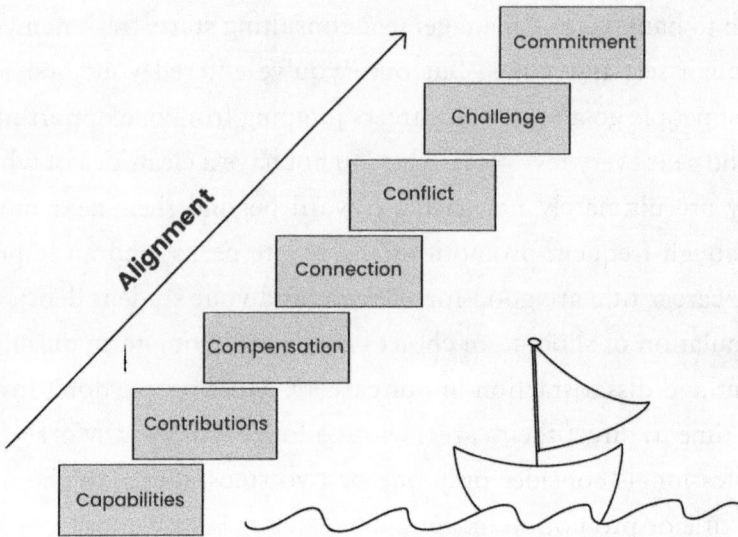

Figure 2.2. The 7 Cs of Work That's Worth It

CAPABILITIES

Your *capabilities* are your advantages—your collection of strengths and skills. Even your values and worldviews are part of your distinct advantages. Knowing your capabilities is how you shine above others. Everyone has a unique combination of talents and lenses through which you see the world that will help you make the change you want to see. Focusing on where you thrive will give you a natural boost as you deliberately lean into your gifts versus focusing on leveling out your weaknesses. It takes continuous effort and self-reflection to understand what you can offer the world, but as you home in on it, you become magnetic to others. You have to cherish what you bring to the table so that others can too. And when you lean into your *capabilities*, it propels you into the Upward Spiral.

CONTRIBUTION

As Mark Twain is rumored to have said, "The two most important days in your life are the day you are born and the day you find out why." Your *contribution* is what can you offer to the world. It becomes your personal mission. It's about giving your time, energy, and talents to something greater than yourself. It's the thread that connects all your experiences. Unfortunately, an emphasis on your contribution is usually missing from your education and often from your career too—especially for professionals entering the private sector. While interviewing for a job at a Fortune 500 company, no one is asking how you would like to contribute to some important issue. They don't often ask, "What about this opportunity has meaning for you?"

You may be drawn into your area of interest due to a personal experience, such as diabetes for Sami Inkinen. Or it may be through a meaningful experience of someone you love. Jane Goodall, for example, developed a deep passion for animals, especially chimpanzees. Her connection to the natural world started when she was a child. From a young age, Goodall displayed a keen curiosity and a deep empathy for animals. She often spent hours observing wildlife, from birds and insects to small mammals. One of the most significant influences on Goodall's connection to nature was her beloved childhood toy, a stuffed chimpanzee named Jubilee (planting the seeds for her future career as a primatologist). Jane Goodall's journey into researching chimpanzees began in 1960, when she traveled to Gombe Stream National Park, in Tanzania, at the invitation of renowned paleontologist Louis Leakey. At the time, Goodall had no formal scientific training, but Leakey believed her patience, curiosity, and empathy made her uniquely suited for studying primates in their natural habitat. Her groundbreaking research on chimpanzees revolutionized our understanding of these animals. By immersing herself in their environment and observing their behavior firsthand, she made several groundbreaking discoveries, including how chimpanzees used tools, a behavior previously believed to be exclusive to humans. This challenged long-held notions about the uniqueness of human intelligence and tool use. Goodall has become not only a pioneering scientist but also a prominent environmentalist and humanitarian. She has used her platform to raise awareness about the importance of biodiversity, conservation, and sustainability, advocating for policies and practices that promote the well-being of both humans and animals.[9]

You can be internally motivated (I need to solve this problem because I have experienced it) or externally motivated (the world needs this problem solved), but most likely, it's a bit of both. It's what you find interesting and enjoy but—more than that—what you make an effort to do, regardless of reward or recognition. Although contributing is about generosity, it also fuels your drive by making you feel great. You may lose track of time while you do it, and in all likelihood, you are willing to fight for it. The best news is that once you find your area of contribution, no one can take it away from you. You can't get fired from your cause.

COMPENSATION

Your *compensation* includes your monetary reward, of course, but it goes well beyond income. It's really about what you receive from the hours you put into your work: it's an exchange of value, and it needs to be balanced over the long term to keep you satisfied, energized, and motivated. There is no shame in wanting to meet your personal desires, such as financial security, looking after your parents, and providing for your current or future family.

Noticing where you are envious of others can indicate that you desire more from your work, and that's okay. We all come from different backgrounds, live in different cities, and are at different stages of life, so our compensation expectations vary greatly, especially over time.

I have observed that most professionals consider compensation in terms of financial gain, versus a more holistic or broader perspective. They may sometimes even miss how they are benefiting from a particular job when they are only calculating the income earned. That can lead to hopping careers and feeling unsatisfied on the other end. Your rewards can also be things like prestige, access to role models or mentors, flexibility at work, breadth of learning available, or satisfaction from the impact of your work. Paying attention and being conscious about how you are compensated is an ongoing process, but it pays off considerably.

Your needs must be met for you to be able to do your best work and to maintain your sense of self-worth. Compensation is important for job satisfaction, but it also lifts a burden from your shoulders (at least financially). When you can worry less about how to care for your family or how you'll pay the rent, you can focus on making a real difference in the world—your contribution. Your compensation returns energy to you, expanding what is possible.

CONNECTIONS

A crucial element for building a career that benefits you and the world is nurturing the *connections* you make along the way. As humans we rely on other humans for everything, ranging from safety to happiness. Your inner circle provides a crucial safety net, supporting you through struggles, offering encouragement, and cushioning your falls.

Beyond that, your broader network—including mentors, colleagues, and others in your field—can act as a trampoline to launch you to new heights and opportunities in your career. You will stand on the shoulders of others who have come before you; thanks to them, you have a head start. And role models and mentors will support and guide you propelling you forward. Teammates will help fill the gaps in your strengths with their strengths to build a complete puzzle of talents. And you're also connected to all your future customers or clients, whose well-being is part of your responsibility. In your area of contribution, you will leave a legacy through the people you later mentor, employ, or inspire to continue spiraling upward.

Whether you're in college or already on your way to building a career, a strong network is essential for your career trajectory regardless of your personality type. The old saying is true: it's not *what* you know; it's *who* you know. According to LinkedIn, 85% of job seekers land positions through connections.[10] Since such a high percentage of jobs are filled via networking of some sort, being highly networked is essential for both the job seekers and for those seeking employees. Also, "not all jobs are publicly advertised. To be exposed to those 'hidden jobs,' you must have a strong online presence on sites like LinkedIn and various job boards so that recruiters can find you."[11] To achieve your career dreams, you don't want to be out of the loop.

CONFLICT

Dealing with conflict, challenges, and setbacks in your career pursuing social good is inevitable. Having difficult conversations and engaging in positive conflict to advance mutual understanding becomes a critical skill, especially as you become a Well-Rewarded

Disruptor who is shaking up the status quo. Learning a framework for conflict can transform tense interactions into opportunities for growth.

It's important to cultivate resilience when faced with obstacles. Respond to rejection humbly and with curiosity, ask for constructive feedback, and be open to possibilities. Addressing self-limiting patterns is just as essential as dealing with external obstacles. Approaching setbacks with positivity and support from others enables perseverance.

CHALLENGE

Many ambitious professionals feel regret later in their careers that they did not aim higher or embrace bigger *challenges* when they were younger and had more time. Having this awareness earlier in your career journey allows you to keep your eyes open for the higher-impact opportunities that interest you. Being more ambitious doesn't necessarily mean working harder or longer hours. Instead, it's about working hard but also smarter—changing the type of work we do so that we can increase our contribution without increasing stress or time commitment. The goal is to move beyond imposter syndrome to thinking big and leaning into the right size challenge for your circumstances.

COMMITMENT

The first six Cs don't mean anything if you don't put them into action. The final C is where ideas become actionable, and it forms a process for building the inertia toward the Upward Spiral for Good. Using your career as a force for good positions you toward becoming a Well-Rewarded Disruptor, connecting your future vision for your personal mission to actionable steps/experiments to get you there. But you have to *commit* and follow through. You must take the first step yourself, then intentionally take every step after that; no one else can do it for you.

Initially in your career, it's rare to feel satisfied with all 7 Cs. However, the important thing is to be aware and intentional with each career move, so that you are always progressing toward your higher purpose. When each of these areas is flourishing individually, they are also interconnected and adding value to the other Cs. For example, when you are building and finding your area of contribution (your personal mission), you are also likely to be building your connections with the people in your work circles that will enhance your contribution.

The better you and your needs are aligned with these seven areas, the more positive those outcomes will be, and the more each piece will feed off the others. It forms a spiral, circling upward as you feel a renewed sense of energy. Ninety thousand hours is a lot of time to be working, and so it's really about the life you are building for yourself to make it worth it, instead of just working a job. Working as a Disruptor for Good creates a rich and fulfilling career, in which you are motivated, disciplined, balanced, and satisfied. It not only supports but also builds your well-being and personal fulfillment, creating positive self-esteem and confidence. Overall you'll feel conscious and present, sustained with passion and creativity, and it will enhance your performance in every area of your life. It allows you to do what you are here to do, in the way you can do it best, and with peace of mind in both your soul and your wallet.

Exercise: Where Are You Now?

You can quickly gauge where you are in your career and where you would like to be on these two simple dimensions: good for you and good for the world. I recommend you do this now before reading further. It will take you less than 5 minutes to complete.

Start by marking a circle along the line on each of the factors below. How satisfied are you with this particular dimension? A response at the far left means you are entirely unsatisfied, and a circle on the far right means you are completely satisfied.

Remember, for a career that's *worth it* you don't need to have both marked all the way to the right to be successful and fulfilled. We naturally understand trade-offs, and what is more important is listening to your needs. Each job is a stepping stone along the journey to finding the right balance.

GOOD FOR YOU?

Are you fulfilled and being rewarded for your work to your satisfaction or desire?

0 _____ 10

GOOD FOR THE WORLD?

Are you satisfied with how your current role contributes positively to the world? In other words, are you landing your magic to have the impact you want?

0 _____ 10

Now do the same exercise again, but this time, mark an X on the same lines above for where you want to be in two years.

Notice what is the same? Are there gaps? This quick test will give you initial insights as to where your attention is needed. Your work will feel *worth it* when you are aligned. It is when your Os and Xs are all on the same point or very close to each other (likely past the halfway point). This is where you can tap into your calling and feel energized by your contribution.

Here is how Grace rated herself when we did this exercise together:

Good for you

0 ——————O ——————— X ——————————————— 10

Good for the world

0 ——————————————————————— O X ————— 10

From this quick exercise, Grace learned that she is content with her contribution. She is not looking to do even more good. However, at this time there is a real gap in how her career is beneficial for her personally. Specifically, she is undercompensated financially for her contribution, and that is leading to burnout. Knowing that she needed to pay attention to how her career is rewarding for her, reminded her to put her needs in the mix. Working through the 7 Cs then allowed her to examine different aspects of her career, broadening the definitions of what is good for her personally so that she could make a more informed decision beyond needing a higher salary. This knowledge motivated Grace to invest the time required to better understand the future she wanted to create for herself so that her ongoing career choices are well thought out and intentional.

⸻

Spiral Upward

When you reach a stage where you are in alignment with what you are doing and where you want to be, you experience fulfillment and empowerment. This energy feeds on itself to create further positivity. That's the Upward Spiral. This is often witnessed by experiencing more ease in your work, the right doors open for you, people coming to you for your expertise, and you feel satisfied with your compensation.

Our careers can contribute positively to the world, and we don't have to sacrifice our financial futures to do it. Grace already had an impactful career, but she needed to get paid more, along with a deeper understanding of how to also gain energy from her contribution. Losing people like Grace to a prestigious well-paying job that is not focused on any positive contribution to the world—other than the ubiquitous but amorphous "providing jobs"—means that the rest of us lose whatever benefit the Graces around us would have created. Instead, we can help her find options that combine her desire for both contribution and compensation.

You can have this too. Finding a true balance ultimately leads to satisfaction in your life and a feeling of significance in your career.

Having worked with many young professionals, I know that the foundation of the 7 Cs is helpful to use as a guide as you think about short- and long-term career decisions and map out a pathway that meets your ambition and fosters continued motivation. With this framework, you can ensure you are navigating in the right direction for you with quarterly check-ins to keep you moving upward on your Spiral.

CHAPTER 3

YOUR CAPABILITIES

What are your unique gifts, and how will you put them to use?

Download the Free Bonuses

If you haven't already done so, it's time to download the companion workbook from my website, or use the following QR code, to capture your thoughts and insights along the way. In addition, you will find other bonuses and resources that go hand in hand with the chapters you are reading that will help you see results faster. I recommend you start by filling in the information you uncover in each exercise directly into the workbook. By the time we finish together, you will have a complete picture of your answers. Use those answers

continued

to assemble your plan for moving forward toward a career that's worth it. It is designed to be a long-term resource for your pathway ahead.

www.workthatsworthit.com/resources

Every human has potential, with talents and strengths that can be harnessed for good, and your unique capabilities can help you make a positive impact on the world. Through self-reflection, experimentation, and intentional choices, we can chart an extraordinary career path that uniquely reflects who we are as individuals, fitting together in harmony with others. Each one of us is unique, and the talents and expertise we offer the world are valuable.

Picture all your life experiences continuously woven into a tapestry, with all different colors and textures. The good, the bad, and the ugly—they all belong there, and they represent who you are and how you show up in the world. Some colors and textures are thicker and more prominent than others. Within this tapestry are threads of your capabilities that encapsulate your values, perspective, strengths, passions, and skills.

Most of us go about our lives with very little awareness of the gems that are woven into our tapestry. Our skills and accolades—the résumé part—may be relatively obvious. But the other threads are the brighter and richer ones that can differentiate you. For all that you engage in during your lifetime, this tapestry comes with you and is always expanding in richness and complexity.

No two tapestries are alike. You are uniquely qualified for what you do—and for what you want to do. No one else has the exact same combination of capabilities. Every person is gifted in multiple ways. We want to unfold how and where you shine, where you stand out from the crowd in not just what you can do but how you think as well. This self-knowledge will lead to a detailed understanding of the value you bring to the table. This clarity of self aligns with the career that only you can do. And that gives you power. It allows you to thoughtfully plan your career instead of taking whatever job you can get. It helps you know your value, so you can negotiate better compensation or advancement. Most of all, it helps you find a career that is specifically meaningful to you, so that you can do the good you want to do in this world. As you reflect on the threads in your tapestry and decide which ones are worth following, make sure that you are open-minded and curious; your path is not always obvious.

If you can tap into your zone of genius, both you and the world benefit. But in reality, it's hard to uncover your capabilities. This is your reminder to start this process and continue it throughout your life. The first step is to identify what is unique and valuable about you. Next, understanding your value will help you present it to others and lean into it. If you can share your advantages overtly and confidently, you get to shape the opportunities in front of you instead of trying to fit into what is already available and leaving important parts of your strengths or perspectives behind.

Taking time to zoom in on the detail of each thread and then zoom

> If you can tap into your zone of genius, both you and the world benefit.

way out to see the overall picture will give you a completely different perspective on your authentic self and how to communicate it. Your unique career will grow from this awareness. Uncovering both a close up and far out view of your capabilities will require some curiosity, vulnerability, and self-reflection on your part. This self-awareness adds to the potency of your work, helping you understand where you can most effortlessly contribute to yourself, your community, and your world. Knowing this may guide you to finding your dream career.

The bottom line is that intentionally applying your uniqueness to your career will lead to greater job satisfaction, higher work engagement, deeper personal well-being, and, as a result, better work performance. As you read this chapter, think about how you are gifted, where you can add value, and what you are doing when you are in a state of flow.

Beyond the Generalist

As a recovering generalist, I understand feeling pressured to diversify and have a portfolio of capabilities. In school and through our careers, we are often encouraged to become a jack-of-all-trades. The idea is that if you're good at a lot of things, you can be open to more opportunities. Early on, sure: keep the doors open while you're exploring and experimenting. But in chasing a wide range of capabilities, we often ignore or abandon what makes our work most impactful. I did this for the first 10 years of my career. I was constantly trying to level out weaknesses by leaning into jobs that challenged me, without noticing that it was taking me further away from my gifts. Looking back, I would have preferred identifying where I added value and stood out; I could have then placed my efforts into enhancing those aspects of myself.

Sure, generalists appear adept at adapting to evolving workplace demands. And most start-ups do require you to hop from one task to another, often drawing upon totally different skills. Through my recent work, I have noticed that transformational people typically specialize, concentrating their effort on accelerating their capabilities instead of forcibly developing myriad skills; it's the difference between playing to win and playing not to lose.

Furthermore, notice your unusual combinations of capabilities and how they come together to make you uniquely valuable. For example, perhaps you are known at your work as a coder—but you are so much more than that. You also stand out as a motivating leader, and you have a knack for politics. Or perhaps you are an artist who also has a keen financial acumen and appreciates structure. Understanding your talent combinations can help you lean into the value you offer.

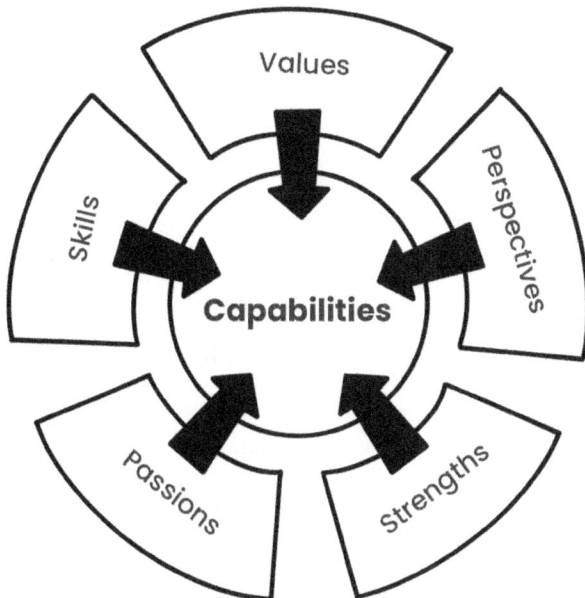

Figure 3.1. Capabilities Portfolio

It is crucial to understand the advantages you can offer the world. The idea is to surface different aspects of who you are, through reflection and exercises, so you can piece together a complete picture of yourself. Let's start with understanding your personal values.

Values

Your values are shaped by your lived experiences. Values are the deeply held beliefs and preferences that shape your choices and guide your behavior. Though often operating subtly in our subconscious, bringing your core values to the surface provides clarity for navigating life's big decisions and filtering the small ones. Understanding your personal values system enables more meaningful, confident, and aligned decision-making. When you know what matters most you can set boundaries, make informed choices, and identify the proper fit. Values may evolve, but knowing yours allows handling inevitable dilemmas through a filter that makes sense to you. Through living in alignment with your values, you gain self-awareness to live authentically, pursue opportunities in harmony with your principles, and filter situations that feel off, so you can respond appropriately.

Many young people I talk to about their careers mention they want to find a company that aligns with their values. That makes sense. However, when I ask them what those values are, they usually can't articulate them easily. That's because we know that our values are contributing subconsciously, but we rarely do the work to bring them to the surface. Their answers can sound like this: "I am looking for a mission-driven company." That makes sense, but it's too vague. It's easy to be more specific. Determining your top three to five values will take you less than 30 minutes.

The same goes for leadership teams. They too usually cannot recite their individual values and can only sometimes easily recall the company values (if they have even been determined). However, every day, the similarities and differences in their values play into their conversations and decision-making. We draw upon our values throughout the day. According to an article in *Psychology Today*, the average adult makes approximately 35,000 decisions per day, averaging 2,000 decisions per hour during your awake hours.[1] Knowing your values will help you get through those thousands of (granted, mostly subconscious) daily decisions more quickly and easily. But more importantly, being able to quickly recite your values will help you in building your career path.

For example, if you know that you value collaboration and an intimate work environment, you'll automatically know working remotely will be challenging for you. If achievement, autonomy, and competition are high on your values list, you know to look for a role that offers little supervision and the chance to run with the ball when it's handed to you. Awareness of your values can also help you know which company or job path you feel most in sync with.

Exercise: Putting Names to Your Top Values

The following is an easy method to determine which words represent your most influential values. In your workbook, start adding in words of values that feel important to you. Remember, there are no right or wrong values, and values do change over time. For example, your values may include honesty, freedom, or creativity; it can be anything. Keep exploring and shoot for at least 30 words (but don't limit yourself). It will take you 20 to 30 minutes to complete.

(Note: in your workbook there is a list of values to consider if you need prompting.)

——————— ——————— ——————— ———————

——————— ——————— ——————— ———————

——————— ——————— ——————— ———————

——————— ——————— ——————— ———————

——————— ——————— ——————— ———————

——————— ——————— ——————— ———————

——————— ——————— ——————— ———————

Then see if the words you have chosen can be grouped by a theme. For instance, if you picked fun, happiness, humor, and joy, these all fit a similar theme. Accountability, transparency, honesty, and responsibility could be part of another grouping. There are no rules for the groupings—it's just what makes sense to you.

Next, if you have more than three to five themes, narrow your selection down to no more than five—all of which have a very powerful resonance and relevance for you. From there, pick the word in each theme that feels right or that encapsulates all the other words, ending up with three to five words. These are your current core values:

——————— ——————— ——————— ———————

Next, write one sentence about each of your top values on how or where you have used this value. That will help you understand whether it's really something that you live by or just an ideal. Feel free to swap something out if you determine a word that resonates better.

The values you have identified are your guideposts, conscious and subconscious. Notice how your values come into play during your days or weeks ahead and make note where you need to change some of the words. For example, if one or more of your values do not show up often in your daily life, make a note of that. You may have selected a value that you respect, but you are not incorporating it into your life yet.

Your core values will shift throughout your life based on your experiences. And that's a positive thing. It means you're continuing to think and question instead of just cruising on autopilot.

The universe has a sense of humor. Along the way, your so-called values will be tested. You will undoubtedly be presented with situations where your values are called into question. Please know that these are not tests that you can fail. They are simply bold opportunities for you to know yourself better and refine your values even further or deeper.

When it comes to values, you will feel more in harmony if you are aligned in and in sync with the people around you. Your overlap may be broader than the five values you selected, but they all feel important and worthwhile to you.

Perspectives

The perspective you bring to the world is important and offers a unique and lived firsthand experience that can be channeled into advantages for the work you pursue.

Your own lens on the world is a precious gift. Our perspective is shaped not just by a single identity or experience but by the intersections of various aspects of our identity (such as race, gender, socioeconomic status, ability, community, and life experience). Acknowledging and exploring these intersections can provide a more nuanced understanding of our unique vantage point.

This viewpoint allows you to see certain problems and solutions—and therefore relate to them—more clearly than others. It steers you toward issues that resonate deeply. Your perspective is what sparks your passions and convictions. It's where you stand, what conclusions you make, what books and articles influence you, what makes you laugh, what makes you cry, what makes you protest and fight, and what is peaceful for you. Without realizing it, we often end up tackling pieces of society's greatest dysfunctions that we can relate to personally. Our perspective points us there.

At the same time, your perspective has blind spots—which is why, when working on a team, you fill in your perspective and your teammates add value with theirs. The combination is what lets the team thrive together. We will likely need to learn to appreciate multiple or opposing perspectives too. When leaning into a career that's *worth it*, striving to identify assumptions and biases in your mind requires humble reflection, but it will help you to weave together alternative perspectives to make more robust decisions. If you make a habit of listening to perspectives different from your own, asking questions, researching diverse viewpoints, and collaborating across lines of difference, even if it is sometimes uncomfortable, it will stretch your thinking. It exposes you to realities you would otherwise miss.

For example, when airbags for automobiles were first introduced as a regular safety feature, they were likely designed by an all-male team, lacking a diverse perspective.[2] Although they were designed as a safety feature, the results showed that women and children were inadequately protected, as the airbag was too strong for their smaller frames upon impact. For almost 20 years, the safety testing was all completed with average male-size dummies. It wasn't until 2009 that female-size dummies were included in the data collection. What this meant is that the risk assessment for women and children was not considered, which resulted in a much higher rate of death or injury for them versus the tested data results.[3] It may not have been deliberate, but with a probable all-male design and testing team, they were probably lacking in the female perspective (or child perspective) to ask about and check the airbag's effects on a smaller body size.

Synthesizing a wide array of perspectives is deeply generative and extremely beneficial in the workforce. It helps you reframe problems and forge innovative solutions. When people with varied lenses work together, combining their diverse strengths, they can achieve exponential impact. As an aspiring leader, bridging differences in perspective helps you guide people, companies, and communities toward a common good. While our perspectives are rooted in our experiences, they are not static. Our perspectives can evolve and shift as we encounter new experiences, knowledge, and people. It's important to remain open to this growth and evolution.

Exercise: Uncovering Your Perspectives through Your Lived Experiences

Take a moment to enter into the workbook your reflections from the following questions. The exercises will surface the perspectives that best highlight what is important to you, and from where you are sitting. It will take you 20 to 30 minutes to complete.

What experiences, identities, or communities have shaped your unique perspective, and how might this perspective enable you to be a champion for certain groups or issues?

_____

_____

What blind spots or biases do you recognize in your perspective, and how might acknowledging these help you better understand and bridge divides with those who have different experiences?

_____

_____

Reflect on significant life experiences (positive or negative) that have impacted your worldview. How could these perspectives help you empathize, innovate, or guide others in your work?

_____

_____

How might your unique perspective allow you to engage diverse stakeholders, bridge divides, or expand people's understanding of a particular issue? What are your gifts or contributions based on this perspective?

_____

_____

Unlike the previous values section, when it comes to perspectives, collaborating with people from different viewpoints is advantageous for your growth, compassion, and broader understanding of your fellow humans. It's also worth noting that some of your lived experiences that add to your perspective can be negatively triggering, and not something that you want to further lean into for your career. These are all choices for you to sort through and make.

Strengths

Strengths are natural traits you're born with and exhibit easily. Sometimes it's where you are naturally gifted, such as artistic talent, athleticism, empathy for others, or being a brilliant mathematician. When using your strengths, you'll notice that the effort you assert feels less draining, and perhaps even energizing. Strengths also often remain constant over time as you draw upon them in different aspects of your life. Less obvious examples include perpetual optimism, innate leadership presence, or a gift for communication. It can be challenging to notice all your strengths, and often what you can see is just an inkling of what lies beneath the surface.

Strengths are often not directly reflected on your résumé or LinkedIn profile, especially if they are what some refer to as *soft skills*. It can be hard to quantify, for example, how you interface with teamwork, your natural leadership style, how you adapt, how coachable you are, how you engage with conflict resolution, what you prioritize, and how you choose to communicate. Strengths play into how you navigate challenges and approach tasks. Determining your own strengths can also be a difficult process, since it's hard to know what is unique or unusual when it's our own normal. We're often much better at seeing strengths in others (this is certainly the case for me). However, this self-awareness will be a crucial skill in revealing your unique capabilities. Identifying them is pivotal for personal and professional growth so that you can lean into them and add skills on top of your strengths. Uncovering them is not just a one-time activity but a lifelong exploration. Understanding your strengths isn't solely about ticking boxes on a test; it's also a nuanced journey.

Exercise: How to Determine Your Strengths

Understanding your strengths requires introspection and external perspectives. The aim is for you to gain a menu of strengths that are in your realm and then to be intentional about which ones you will put your energy behind.

Start by simply asking the people around you. You can kick this task off with a few quick texts by tapping into the insights of the people you trust. Ask them: "How would you describe my strengths?" "What is unique about me?" "Where do I stand out?" This exercise not only reveals external perceptions but also provides a mirror reflecting your strengths through the eyes of those who know you well.

Ask your friends and family; your coworkers; your old teachers, professors, or coaches; and your mentors. What would they identify as your unique gifts? It's even better if they can give an example. Keep the conversation informal, so they keep it honest. The tough part of doing this is getting past feeling self-conscious. But it will be informative and useful, and you are wisely seeking more awareness about how you can tap into your values and use them in your future endeavors.

The most important piece of this exercise is to be open to really listening. Stay curious, and ask questions if you want to better understand what that person means. Ideally, ask more than five people, and put all their comments on one page so you can refer to them when you need a confidence boost. The time this test will take will depend on whether you are sending a quick text versus having a longer conversation. Add the feedback to your workbook.

My strengths

_____

What is unique about me

_____

Where I stand out

_____

~~~~

STRENGTHS ASSESSMENTS

Another option is to dive into the world of structured strength assessments to gain a more systematic understanding of your strengths. You may not need a formal test, but I like throwing these in the mix because they usually help you gain new insights. I find strength tests especially relevant for my clients when they are surrounded by a lot of people with the same skills, when they are unaware that they stand out because of the pool of similar exceptional talent. Additionally, it can also be difficult to identify your own strengths when you are in an environment that does not value them. For example, say your family values competition, but you are naturally collaborative. It may take a while before you understand and utilize this strength. Or perhaps you have been raised to people-please, becoming highly adaptable in service of others—overshadowing where you can add the most value to the world.

My first recommendation would be the Values in Action (VIA) Character Survey (the name is confusing; it's not about values).[4] I like it because it's straightforward and only takes about 15 minutes of your time. It also adds in a bunch of words to your strengths list that are not normally included without this prompt. I took the test a few years ago and was surprised to find that my number one strength is my love of learning. I didn't realize then that this was a strength I should pay attention to and utilize in my work life. But upon reflection it made 100% sense to me, and it is why I am always in situations where I am learning and growing. Since then, I have understood that whatever I'm working on needs to incorporate some sort of learning component to keep me most engaged and connected to where I add value.

The three assessments you see most often in the corporate world are the CliftonStrengths Assessment, the Myers-Briggs Type Indicator Assessment, and the Enneagram Personality Test.[5] These assessments are just a chance to look in the mirror and see what feels right for you; their answers are not a diagnosis or facts. You may not fit perfectly into a category, and these tests may not accurately reflect how you see yourself. Pay attention to the parts that resonate with you and where you feel aligned, and let go of the rest. We also all change throughout life, and these assessments capture how you respond to questions at one moment in time (even if they claim to not change with retesting). So take the career suggestions related to these assessments with a grain of salt. They are usually very linear translations of the strengths that are exposed by answering their questions, and they don't include future work strengths that we can't predict or imagine. The bottom line is that you are one of a kind and so much more than a label. Try not to get hung up on the results, but use the answers to build a more informed picture about what you bring to the table.

Whatever assessment or tool you use, add your findings to your workbook. The workbook also includes codes to easily find and take the tests.

Notice where you stand out, and get comfortable sharing your strengths with others. Also, look at what strengths are emerging. They may not be your top strengths right now, but depending upon the circumstances in your life they may become more prominent later, especially in combination with your skills (which you will outline later).

Passions

Having a genuine passion—the kind that completely absorbs you— is a magical experience. It starts with an insistent curiosity and can quickly develop into a deep interest. In many cases, it can drive you forward with relentless momentum. Time seems to melt away when you are fully immersed, lost in the joyful creative flow state. You can hyperfocus and become dead to most distractions. It's like falling into a trance where greater powers take over. Days, weeks, or even longer spans of time seem to disappear, and the passion dominates every waking thought.

For some people, their passions can overlap with their career path. It is obvious how that provides you with a supercharged advantage. It's the kind of passion that can last a lifetime. Overlaying the necessary discipline on top of that passion does not kill it. It gives it structure and a pace that makes it possible to endure obstacles along the way.

Notably, passions are not always suited for our careers. Some passions cannot easily be monetized and are more for enjoyment. And other times, spending all day in your one area of passion can extinguish your love for it.

Passions are powered by intrinsic rewards well beyond your paycheck. Following them, especially when they build value for others, leads to greater well-being. For example, I am passionate about companies doing amazing work that contributes positively to the world. I read about them every day, I watch documentaries on them, and I tell others about them. Your passion doesn't necessarily have to involve a skillset but can also be an area of consistent and deep interest: the environment, for example, or women's rights. Having a specific interest or knowledge base adds to your capabilities.

Exercise: Revealing Your Passions

Answer the following questions. It will take you 20 to 30 minutes to complete.

What activities, subjects, or topics genuinely excite you and captivate your interest, even in your free time? When have you experienced a state of complete engagement or flow while pursuing these interests?

_____

_____

Do you have any passions or areas of expertise that others often seek your advice or knowledge about? How might these passions contribute value to the world or your potential career path?

_____

_____

Reflect on the passions you've identified. Can you envision sustaining these passions for an extended period (say, 10 years)? Would pursuing them professionally fuel or potentially diminish your enthusiasm? How might you monetize or apply these passions in a way that aligns with your values and goals?

_____

_____

After answering these first three questions, do you have any passions that you want to carry forward with you into your work?

_____

_____

If you do indeed have a passion that you can incorporate into your career, staying engaged and developing expertise becomes automatic. Most people struggle to incorporate passion into their work, so you're not alone if you have not surfaced something to weave into your career.

Skills

Most career advisors start with your skills and help you find your career path (better described as your *skills path*), overlooking all the other capabilities we have already explored previously. Your name is allocated to a job title, which refers to a skillset you will perform. This mindset is largely driven by the efficiency of filling an open job as quickly as possible, getting the tasks done for the systems to operate smoothly. But it undermines what makes us beneficially human. It's influenced by the Industrial Revolution, where humans had to fill jobs as if they were robots. In larger companies, your performance will be tracked by software to optimize your time and skills efficiency. And guess what: today, robots have already come for these roles (or are coming), and for any repeatable or predictable task they're likely to outperform us all.

If you are someone who needs to combine meaning and ambition in your work and you excel in an environment where you are able to show up as your full human self, building a career on skills will not likely be fulfilling over the long term. However, the phrase "it's the skills that pays the bills" is accurate too. Skills are useful and important in your career, but as we spend more hours in the workforce, what you are really doing is building a portfolio of expertise (which includes a subset of skills). Furthermore, to launch you into your Upward Spiral, combining your skills with the topics addressed earlier (perspective, values, strengths, and passions) is how you become known for something and build a legacy.

Let's take a look at your skills and find out how they are adding value to your career, beyond employability. Your skills are your developed abilities, learned through education, repetition, training, and experience. Professionally speaking, skills are the keywords we list on our résumés that we acquire through education and job experiences. They can be easily explained and demonstrated. For example, public speaking can be attained through deliberate effort or coding skills achieved through computer science courses. Skills also encompass certifications, credentials, specializations, and micro-skills that set you apart. Skills capture competencies you actively hone and leverage to excel professionally.

You can determine your professional skills by taking inventory of what you do and the recognition you've earned. To put your list together, start with any degrees for education you have received—both traditional education and any online courses you have completed (especially the ones that offered a certification). From there, think about all the tangible skills that you have learned in any work experience you have had. Do you know how to perform a particular role at a company, such as product management? Or have you mastered the use of a particular software, such as Salesforce?

There are many different organizations offering skills assessments, but LinkedIn is a great first stop. If you are not sure of the skills you have developed, do a search on LinkedIn for someone with a similar job title and industry, and see what they list on their profile; you may share some of those skills. Build out your list of the skills you have.

LinkedIn keeps a running list of skills that job seekers should have—for example, "The Most In-Demand Skills" include communication, customer service, and leadership at the top of the list. Adaptability is also noted as their top skill of the moment. But these vary year by year, and with artificial intelligence (AI) advancing so fast, the skills needed in the market are changing fast. Look on LinkedIn's blog for the latest. In addition, the World Economic Forum (WEF) has a list of top skills that currently include creativity, complex problem-solving, and active learning.[6]

Exercise: Tangible Skills

Take a few minutes to write down the answers to these questions:

Based on your education, work experiences, and personal interests, what tangible skills have you developed so far? Which of these skills energize you and contribute to your success? If you have a résumé, start by looking at your job titles.

_____   _____   _____   _____

_____   _____   _____   _____

Reflecting on the skills you've identified, which ones do you want to continue nurturing and building expertise in? Are there any skills that may become obsolete due to technological advancements like AI, and how can you adapt or develop complementary skills? Record your thoughts.

_____

_____

_____

_____

UP- OR RESKILLING

Don't forget adaptability, and your willingness to pivot and change. With the rapid insertion of AI into the employment equation, some 50% of all employees will need some level of reskilling.

For example, if you have been in the energy sector working in fossil fuels, it's time to reskill into renewable energy. In 2023, the WEF included in its "Future of Jobs" report that in the next five years around 44% of today's jobs will be disrupted.[7] This means that flexibility, creativity, learning capacity, resilience, stress tolerance, and problem-solving will all be at a premium.

In your career, constant upskilling will need to be part of your career journey, allowing you to expand and adapt your professional toolkit. But instead of upskilling, let's think of it as *expertise deepening*. You might think of skills as crucial to getting a job, and they often are. But they can also be learned or improved on the job. Much more important is your mindset, your drive, and your unique, combined set of capabilities.

There are many avenues for upskilling or reskilling. If you're currently employed, your company may offer you upskilling benefits as part of your compensation. Aside from that, there are easily accessible courses and certificates on any given skill that can keep you relevant to the current job demand. LinkedIn, Google, and many other platforms offer free and paid upskilling options, along with traditional universities. Please note that you don't want to be forever chasing skills as you run from AI. Take the time to really think what can be useful alongside AI. What skills will enhance your expertise that you can offer the world that is not replicable? As someone who has a love of learning, reskilling is part of who I am in order to stay engaged. Being committed to your growth and adding valuable threads to your tapestry is always going to be helpful.

As roles evolve much faster than ever before, learning to upskill or reskill becomes a critical part of your career plan. It also boosts engagement as you feel continually upskilled, not obsolete.

Exercise: Skills I Am Considering Developing through Upskilling and Reskilling

This will take you 20 to 30 minutes to complete.

Based on your current skills, career aspirations, and the evolving job market demands, what new skills or areas of expertise do you want to cultivate or enhance? List these skills or areas of expertise in your workbook and answer how might these skills contribute to your overall professional growth and ability to navigate your career path.

_____

_____

_____

_____

_____

_____

For each skill or area listed, research the potential learning resources, courses, programs, or certifications available. While considering your resources, reflect on your learning style and preferences. How can you incorporate upskilling or reskilling into your routine sustainably and engagingly, such as with online courses, workshops, mentorships, and on-the-job training? Estimate the time commitment and potential costs involved. Fill in your answers in the workbook.

Skill	Resource	Time commitment	Cost

Which ones from this list would you like to prioritize first?

_____

Consider potential mentors, industry experts, or professional networks that could provide guidance, support, or opportunities for upskilling or reskilling in your desired areas.

_____

_____

~~~

Exercise: Crafting Your Capability Statement

Throughout this chapter, you've delved into various facets that make up your unique set of capabilities: your values, perspective, passions, skills, and strengths. Now it's time to synthesize these elements into a concise yet powerful statement that captures the essence of who you are, where you are going, and the value you bring with you.

OPTION 1: DESCRIPTIVE SENTENCES

Imagine a mentor introducing you to a potential employer, collaborator, or colleague who wants to understand what makes you unique. In two or three sentences, how will they holistically describe you in a way that highlights the most significant aspects of your capabilities? This step will take around 30 minutes, drawing upon your previous answers.

If you need ideas to get started, consider the following prompts to build your description:

- What are your core values and how do they shape your approach?
- What is your unique perspective or lens on the world?
- What passions drive and energize you?
- What are your key strengths and areas of expertise?
- How do these elements combine to create a distinct value proposition?

_____

_____

_____

_____

_____

_____

OPTION 2: WORD CLOUD

Create a visual representation of your capabilities by assembling a word cloud or bubble diagram. Include keywords or short phrases that capture the key perspectives, values, passions, skills, and strengths you want to highlight. Arrange and size the words or phrases in a way that reflects their relative importance or emphasis, or underline anything you want to stand out first and foremost. This process will also take around 30 minutes drawing upon your answers earlier.

Impact

Curiosity Entrepreneurship

Love of Learning

Marketing

Relationships

Listening **Integrity**

Author **Thought Leader**

Podcaster

Empathy **Courage**

Global

Figure 3.2. Capabilities Word Cloud

Once you've crafted your capability statement or word cloud, take a moment to reflect on how it resonates with you. Does it accurately capture the unique combination of elements that make you who you are? If not, revise and refine it until you feel it truly represents your authentic self. Remember, these exercises are not about fitting into a predetermined mold or job description. It's about celebrating the richness of your capabilities and recognizing the value you can bring to the world when you align your work with your true essence.

Each time you recognize an advantage, you can now weave it into your tapestry, which fosters a more comprehensive and nuanced self-awareness to add to your professional journey.

This strategic advantage allows you to craft a career path that aligns with your authentic self. It provides clarity in choosing roles where your contributions are not only valued, but celebrated as well. As you lean into your capabilities, you become a more impactful and fulfilled professional, contributing meaningfully to your workplace and community.

You Are So Much More than Any Job Description

Sadly, your résumé or LinkedIn profile leaves out so much about why you are valuable. And your unique capabilities go well beyond your job description or title. By expanding your perspective on your own capabilities, you'll uncover a treasure trove of talents that contribute to your uniqueness. Expanding your capabilities stack never stops in a truly fulfilling career.

I want you to feel proud and excited about who you are. I want you to be able to communicate your capabilities to others in a way that is not salesy or boastful, but instead as a confident offering to the world. I want you to be able to look at your job choices and understand how much or little of your gifts will get to shine in that job. I want you to know who can complement your skills and strengths. And I want you to feel empowered in your career to achieve your ambitions.

Imagine most people are riding up a hill on a regular bike, and when you are in your zone, you have an e-bike. You're still riding up and down hills, but your effort allows you to go farther faster, with more ease and enjoyment. Certainly, 90,000 hours is a long time and having clarity of your gifts allows you to keep going for the long haul.

It takes a lot of work to be self-reflective. But if you're like Grace and want to contribute to the world in a positive way, understanding your capabilities is an essential building block to getting to the upper right quadrant faster and better. And through this work, you will be able to authentically differentiate yourself from the vast majority of professionals as people do not invest their time in doing so.

Eventually most of us find our zone of genius, and sometimes adults later in their careers finally find themselves as a Well-Rewarded Disruptor. However, I don't believe we have to wait until retirement to tap into our gifts, and I'm interested in getting you there earlier in your career cycle through intentionality. Nurturing your capabilities is something we can all learn to do. Plus, our planet needs it! And it will make your life more interesting too.

YOUR NEXT BIG MOVER

As you reflect on the insights and exercises from this chapter, consider the following: What is one powerful step you can take—a big move you can make—to align your capabilities with the valuable work you want to do in the world? This is your Big Mover for the chapter—an intentional leap you can take to move toward becoming a Well-Rewarded Disruptor. For example, you might decide that your Big Mover is to pick one capability and measurably improve it. This Big Mover could be a mindset shift, a commitment to developing a particular strength, or a tangible action that allows you to lean into your values or passions more deeply. It might feel like a stretch, but that's often where growth and transformation reside.

What Big Mover action could propel you closer to utilizing your unique gifts in service of creating positive impact? Take a moment to capture your Big Mover in your workbook or the following.

_____

_____

_____

_____

CHAPTER 4

YOUR CONTRIBUTION

What are you here to do in the world?

DO YOU REMEMBER EAGER ADULTS sizing you up and asking when you were in high school: "What do you want to be when you grow up?" and then "What do you want to do after college?" Such simple, standalone questions beg simple answers like "lawyer," "marketing," or "operations." But did anyone ever dream of "operations" when they were a child? Does the answer give you any real insight into what is important to them, who they are, and what they value? And it doesn't stop later either. "What do you do for work?" is often one of the first questions any American will ask within 10 minutes of meeting you for the first time. Did you set out to spend your 90,000 career hours doing only "accounting"? What if we asked each other, "What is so important to you that you *have* to do it?" or "What do you care about in the world?" or "What would you love to change about the world?"

Amy Wrzesniewski, a professor at the Yale School of Management, has spent her career exploring how individuals relate to their work. Basically, it can be boiled down to three approaches. She's found that people either have a job, a career, or a calling.[1]

Most people experience a job at some point in their life. It's as a cashier or working at the ice-cream store during your summer break. Maybe it's how you pay the rent right after high school or college. You probably don't feel emotionally connected with the company or the products it sells, but it provides a paycheck and maybe some benefits. There is little chance of significant promotion, and you accept that is part of the role. It's easy to quit with two weeks' notice, and both you and your boss know that the company can easily replace you at any time. Meaning in your life is likely to come outside of work.

Next up the pyramid is the career-oriented professional who is willing to put in long hours each week, climbing the corporate ladder. You have long-term goals and ambition for yourself in a particular arena, such as sales or marketing or IT. You may start at the bottom, but you seek opportunities to further your skillset and work your way to progressively higher-paid, more responsible positions. You are still replaceable in this work category, but if you put in the hours, you will leave your mark. Careers are also known as *elevator jobs*—jobs that have the potential to move you up.

Then there is the calling. It's rare and deeply rewarding—even magical. Your work fits well into your most cherished values and taps into where you are a genius. The more you achieve at work, the more motivated and committed you become, frequently overcoming enormous obstacles. Because of your passion for what you do, because of your commitment to the company's vision and goals (or your own vision and goals if you're an entrepreneur or solopreneur), very little can stand in your way! You feel dedicated, fulfilled, admired, and deeply satisfied, and your passion is contagious and powerful, uplifting those around you.

Not surprisingly, Wrzesniewski's research shows that as people move up from a job to a career to a calling, so does job satisfaction as these workers "are more likely to 'craft' their jobs to fit their strengths and interests."[2]

Let's take a look at an entrepreneur's winding path to finding her calling. Debbie Sterling's journey to becoming a Disruptor for Good is a testament to the power of a personal mission and the unexpected ways our experiences can shape our calling. As a Stanford engineering graduate in 2005, Debbie didn't immediately find her path. Instead, her route to founding GoldieBlox—a company dedicated to closing the gender gap in STEM fields through toys and animation—was marked by curiosity, diverse experiences, and a willingness to follow her instincts.[3]

After graduation, Debbie's career took several seemingly unrelated turns. She experimented in various roles early in her career, each adding a unique perspective to her growing toolkit, but nothing felt quite right. To shake things up, Debbie said yes to an opportunity to join a volunteer program in rural India for six months. As is often the case with life adventures, her experience in India opened her mind as she gained a broader perspective, and in the process, she learned that a not-for-profit life was not her long-term calling.

She returned back to the US wiser, but seemingly even more lost in her career. However, her constant optimism and adventurous spirit led her to apply for a position at a small jewelry design company after spotting an opening on LinkedIn. While jewelry wasn't her passion, this role provided crucial on-the-job training and insights into running a small business—knowledge that would later prove essential for her own start-up (she even refers to those years as her "paid MBA").

The seeds of GoldieBlox were planted long before Debbie even realized it. Her experiences as a Girl Scout in her youth, the scarcity of female classmates in her engineering program at Stanford, exposure to design thinking and iterative processes, and even hearing Steve Jobs speak about passion at her college graduation all contributed to shaping her personal mission.

The catalyst for GoldieBlox came during an "ideas monthly brunch" Debbie organized with colleagues, where she had her "aha" moment, recognizing the need for STEM toys designed specifically for girls. She was uniquely qualified to shake things up in that arena. Debbie's hypothesis was simple yet powerful: by exposing young girls to science, technology, engineering, and mathematics through play at a young age, she could inspire them to pursue STEM fields later in life.

Today, GoldieBlox has evolved from a toy company into a children's multimedia group, offering books, apps, and content that make STEM accessible and appealing to young girls (and boys). The company has partnered with Random House Children's Books and even created STEM engineering badges for the Girl Scouts, bringing Debbie's journey full circle.

Turning Problems into Possibilities

Young professionals today care more than ever before about the environmental and social issues related to the work they do. Yes, there are lots of people who only focus on what's in it for themselves, but I am optimistic that this category is shrinking. They are not my low-hanging fruit to channel into careers that positively impact our world. Companies are starting to pay attention to this trend, which is evidenced by how they allure young recruits highlighting their sustainable practices and how they are marketing their goods and services to their end customers and deliberately highlighting their impact. Directionally, we are course correcting—but perhaps not fast enough.

You'll recall that the four extremes of doing good in the world are on two axes: "good for you" on one axis, and "good for the world" on the other side. I created this diagram to better understand where my coaching clients were coming from when they felt frustrated or at a roadblock at work. It may be oversimplified, but it really helps narrow down whether we need work on finding a way for you to benefit more from work or whether we need your work to have greater meaning. Grace, for example, felt satisfied with her contribution. However, after digging deeper with her regarding the "good for you" piece, she was unclear about what she really wanted to achieve with her career—the big picture. Each role she had in the early start of her career offered terrific experience, skills, and contacts, but after several years, that benefit held less value. Not having a clear picture of how she wanted to apply her talents—and to what cause—left her feeling demotivated.

This is your opportunity to dive deep into the positive impact your career can have. We each have the opportunity to be mindful of where our energy and time go. You have heard the saying: "The grass is greener on the other side." Well, there is another related saying that is relevant to where we choose to allocate our work hours: "The grass is greener where you water it." It goes back to intention and how you will spend your career hours. What we spend time cultivating grows, so choose wisely.

10,000 Feet above the Ground

If problems are on one side of a coin, the other side offers solutions. For some people, it's easier to connect with the problem. For others, it's the solutions that excite them. It's not important what draws you in; they are equally helpful. It just depends on what works for you. Normally, both are useful motivators. Between these two ends are the possibilities.

Debbie Sterling's journey hasn't been without challenges. Despite her Stanford engineering degree and her role in founding a STEM-focused company, she's faced pushback from some who challenge her right to call herself an engineer. Along the way she often faced imposter syndrome. Her solution: she leaned into her passion and curiosity, which was greater than her fear. Her cause meant so much to her that she pushed through. These experiences have underscored the importance of self-worth and staying focused on her mission, even in the face of criticism.

Debbie's story reinforces a crucial message: you get to choose your calling and what you care about in the world. If you encounter skepticism or attempts to discredit you, lean into your self-worth and continue your work. You don't need a specific degree, permission, or even a perfect idea to have a positive impact in our world. If you have an inkling of where you'd like to invest your time and energy, keep following those breadcrumbs.

Fueling this journey is the tangible impact of Debbie's work. She saves letters from young women in STEM who have been inspired by GoldieBlox toys or content, using them as motivation during challenging times. These testimonials serve as powerful reminders of the real-world impact of her mission. That is typical as a Disruptor for Good; achieving success goes beyond their specific balance sheet of your company. As you read about problems you may be interested in solving, think through the possible solution ideas and what that makes possible for the industry. Where, within those pieces, would you like to contribute toward?

To understand the macro view of what the world needs, the World Economic Forum's report *Global Risks Perception Survey 2024* cites the following top areas of concern the world is likely to face over the coming 10-year period: censorship and surveillance, critical change to Earth systems, the concentration of strategic resources, erosion of human rights and civic freedoms, inequality or lack of economic opportunity, intrastate violence, and talent and labor shortages.[4] These are all global megatrends that are challenging to solve and require more human attention. You may have other local issues that your community is facing, which are equally important. As you consider the bigger picture of what the world needs, imagine yourself building expertise in a topic that is important to you. Is there something that already pulls at you?

Your Personal Mission

Let's go back to Grace for a moment. She is contributing to a range of meaningful problems that are worth solving through her work, including healthcare in Africa, women's health, finance in healthcare, and poverty. However, she has never considered finding her own calling and letting it guide her choices. So although she feels good about and is stimulated by the work she is doing, it is not *her* calling. She does not even know what hers is yet. And that may be a contributing factor in how she is feeling under-rewarded for her great work; when you are in a state of flow within your own personal mission, it generates energy.

My intention is to get people to embrace a meaningful and rewarding career contributing positively to the world. Grace definitely checks that box under anyone's measures. But I also want her to last 90,000 hours to add value to our world and feel rewarded for her work, making her career worth her investment of time and energy. Looking after herself is just as important. Making a contribution is great; making *your* contribution toward *your* calling is life-changing. I have witnessed that people who have found a calling that fuels their career helps them enter and then stay in our top quadrant: the Well-Rewarded Disruptor. As you may remember, Grace is considering pausing her contribution for more money, which won't get her to this quadrant in the short term and may jeopardize her happiness in the long term.

> # Making a contribution is great; making *your* contribution toward *your* calling is life-changing.

Debbie's personal mission has guided her decisions ever since founding her company GoldieBlox, and has kept her motivated for over a decade. She remains passionate about exposing girls to their STEM potential from an early age. As she puts it, entrepreneurs need to "be obsessed" and relentless with their personal mission to overcome the inevitable obstacles and stay true to their vision.

Debbie's success isn't just about her idea; it's also about her unique capabilities. She describes one of her superpowers as the ability to bridge creative ideas with execution—a rare combination of right-brain and left-brain thinking. She's comfortable articulating and leveraging her strengths, which include innovative thinking, the ability to connect big-picture vision with day-to-day tasks, and a knack for charming and connecting with people. Her wins at GoldieBlox are from her talent to recognize when someone aligns with her mission and seize those opportunities for collaboration.

In full disclosure, I have experienced a common resistance from my coaching clients to committing to a theme or topic for their personal contribution (except for those already in the Well-Rewarded Disruptor zone). The others are more comfortable committing to traditional job verticals such as finance or customer relations than something they care deeply about such as clean oceans or refugees. They have shared that "It's already hard to find a job" or "I am not sure I want to dedicate my life to that," pushing back on the concept. And fair enough; there is nowhere to search for jobs that support refugees. Those answers are normal if you too are feeling hesitant. The terms "find your calling" and "discover your purpose" also seem daunting to my clients. Through experimentation, using the words "building your personal mission" lowers anxiety for most people, especially when we talk about crafting and refining it over time. Companies have missions, so why can't you? And they can be tweaked and adjusted as needed or circumstances change. Regardless of whether you are feeling weary or excited, let's try and see what surfaces for you, as each intentional step will get you closer to your zone of genius.

Can you open yourself up to consider the following: "What personal mission would make sense for me?" or "What can I try on as my personal mission for my career?" It is a little like finding a partner to share your life with. It may take 50 first dates. But you know when something lights you up. However, the better you know yourself, the greater your chances of getting the direction right earlier in your journey. Also like finding a partner, your personal mission must be a unique fit for you and must involve contributing to a problem you truly believe is important and worthy of your time. And it requires taking the first step and being open to experiment.

The first stage of discovery is to get the juices flowing about what are some of the important topics that you care about, plus what big problems in the world you may want to help solve. In this stage, there are two reflective exercises, and you should do both. Next, in stage 2, you will narrow your list down to one or two overarching words that can navigate the direction of your contribution. These words can be as broad or specific as you feel comfortable. They will act as a compass. For now, you may feel comfortable settling into this stage before moving on to stage 3. The final stage is when you are ready to make a bold declaration regarding your personal mission. If you are already a Well-Rewarded Disruptor or have clarity about your contribution, you can jump ahead here. This stage helps you lean into your calling, as Wrzesniewski describes earlier. After completing these exercises, you will also end up with a short personal mission statement that will help you communicate to others what you care about. You can go all the way now or come back to stage 3 when you are ready and have more clarity.

Exercise Stage 1: Two Steps

This two-step process helps you surface a list of relevant topics that are important to you that you can draw upon for inspiration. It's best to do these exercises when you are well-rested and relaxed, accessing a calm and deeper level of thinking. Spend time brainstorming both the bottom-up or top-down exercises; we will look at both to see what surfaces. When completed, you will reflect on how to link the lists.

BOTTOM-UP APPROACH

Beginning the journey of building your unique personal mission often connects to the positive and negative experiences that have shaped you. Our lives unfold in chapters, some joyful, others painful, all of them influencing our life journey. Reflecting on pivotal moments and emotions helps reveal the lenses through which we see the world, shaping our thoughts and clarifying our values. Through these experiences, you can discover what matters to you. That self-understanding helps us gravitate toward a personal mission that is relevant and valuable.

With that in mind, brainstorm and answer the following questions drawing upon some powerful experiences from your life. This step will take you 20 to 30 minutes to complete.

What experiences in your life left you feeling delighted, valued, successful, or proud? From your list, what do you wish others could feel or experience too?

_____

_____

_____

What brought deep pain or hardship? What challenges do you hope to help others avoid?

_____

_____

_____

_____

What still leaves you feeling regret or lack of fulfillment? What problems break your heart?

_____

_____

_____

Wrestling with these questions surfaces powerful themes (which can take some time to understand). They point to where we find motivation and purpose. In honoring those good or bad life experiences lies your wisdom. Uncovering where our capabilities and contributions intersect with the unmet needs in your community, or globally will bring meaning to your life. Our susceptibility to these issues reveals their urgency.

Write down your reflection on the themes, or how you can connect your ideas from the previous three lists in your workbook or here. Also, capture why these themes or topics mean something to you. We will go back to them later in the chapter:

_____

_____

_____

_____

TOP-DOWN APPROACH

Let's think about what the world needs regardless of whether it's a local community need or global. If you had a magic wand and could solve a meaningful problem anywhere in the world, what would that be? What problem or possibility in the world is the most important to you or gets you consistently fired up? What is worth your time? What podcasts do you love listening to? What topics do you always follow up on? Does our warming atmosphere, rising seas, and increasingly frequent and extreme storm systems keep you up at night? Are you constantly thinking about how you might help the underrepresented find their voice? Are you fascinated by technology and intrigued by the possibilities of renewable energy? Whatever is most important to you, that's a theme you will feel energized leaning into.

Write down a list of topics you would like to play a part in. What is it that you deeply care about that you could spend the next five to 10 years working on (or more)? It may be something you would love to see grow into something bigger. Or something you can't stand that you want to see changed. It's okay if there are several areas you find important; that's normal. Write them all down. I've added a few to get you started, but these should be issues you feel drawn to within yourself, not problems you—or anyone else—think you *should* care about. (Note: often, the closer you are to the problem, the more motivated you will be to work on the solution.) This step will take you 15 minutes to complete.

IF I HAD A MAGIC WAND I WOULD . . .

- Amplify Indigenous voices
- Offer health as a right to all humans
- Provide equity, representation, and safety to any underrepresented group
- End fossil fuels and transition to renewables

- _____
- _____
- _____
- _____
- _____
- _____
- _____
- _____

You're not limited to this list; it's just a big-picture start. But just from that short list, is there anything that feels urgent to you? Something that makes you feel alive? That speaks to you? Something that is not a fleeting interest, but something you can care about for many years to come? Take a moment to understand why you are connected to these topics. We're not talking specifics— just your feelings around big overarching issues and ideals.

COMBINING THE LISTS

What have you learned about yourself from these two lists so far? Can you connect the dots between any on the bottom-up list to the top-down list? What would you like to be known for on your lists? Or for what topics would you be excited to build deep expertise? Write down your thoughts, and we will draw upon this for stage 2. This step requires some deeper thinking and may take you 30 minutes to capture your thoughts.

_____

_____

_____

_____

Next, answer these questions too that draw upon why a particular topic matters to you.

How do these topics connect to my own life experiences or impact me (if any)?

_____

How would working on this topic be fulfilling?

_____

Next, you have a choice. If you are thinking about your desired contribution for the first time, go to stage 2 next, where we will narrow down your focus and get you going.

On the other hand, if you already have a lot of clarity about your contribution, you can skip straight to stage 3 and get your personal mission statement written and ready to declare to the world.

Exercise Stage 2: Just One or Two Words

With the bottom-up and top-down exercises we have already gone through, you now have some ideas of what may draw you in. Now we are ready to get you moving in a direction that is meaningful to you. Let's narrow down your contribution to a theme word or two, like you would for a New Year's resolution. This should take 10 minutes or so of your time.

What one word speaks to you? The word can be simple—such as *women, environment, safety, equity, joy,* or even your home country or another region of the world you care deeply for.

My word is _____.

Or combine two words. For example, you might pair *refugees* with *dignity, art* with *activism, AI* and *ethics,* or *Mexico* with *climate change.* This narrows your initial one-word calling by connecting it with some outcome, location, or other important cause.

My two words are _____ and _____.

This simple word strategy can help guide you significantly during your early years developing your career, and you can refine your impact area as you go along. Just get started and the rest will take shape. The most important message I hope to land with you in this chapter is for you to include your personal mission into your career journey. Let that be what connects your different experiences and provides you with the motivation and grit needed for a career that's worth it.

You can now more profoundly answer the following conversation starter: "What do you do for a living?" Practice answering . . .

My career contributes toward bettering _____,

I am helping solve _____, or

I am changing _____.

~~~~~

Exercise Stage 3: Ready to Declare Your Personal Mission

Figuring out your personal mission will take more clarity, and perhaps a deeper understanding of what is important to you specifically. Some people just have that deep sense of clarity, and that's wonderful (like Greta Thunberg). Others need to open themselves up to uncovering and building it slowly, and that works too—it's a journey.

In Chapter 2 we read about Sami Inkinen from Virta Health. His personal mission is to end diabetes and obesity in 1 billion people. It is also Virta's mission because he founded the company based on his desired contribution. It's clear and easily retold by a colleague, friend, or journalist. Learning about his personal mission is so much more telling than his title as CEO, or a health tech entrepreneur. To capture the essence of this exercise, allocate 30 minutes.

The goal of this stage is to declare your personal mission. Here are two suggested ways you can get yours in words:

"I help/achieve/protect/initiate (what you do) _____

by (how you do it) _____ because (why you do it)

_____ ."

"I will (what you will accomplish) _____ by (when)

because (why you do it) _____ ."

Your personal mission can be specific or general—whatever helps serve you as a guiding force. Examples include, "My personal mission is to catalyze the transition to clean energy by accelerating renewable energy adoption and innovation because I'm committed to mitigating climate change and creating a sustainable future for generations to come." Or, if you are still exploring your "how," your statement could look like this: "My career is dedicated to fostering women's equality. I'm not sure yet what aspect of that work intrigues me most, but I'm assessing my options and figuring that out." Can you feel the power in those statements, the thoughtfulness, maturity, and relevance? Once you know what you care about in the world, you can direct your career toward the kind of day-to-day work you'd like to do.

Exercise: Personal Mission Check-In for Stage 2 and 3

Once you have a personal mission that excites you, run it through the following questions to see if it can stand the test of time and interest for you over the long term. It will take 5 minutes.

- Can you easily articulate how this makes the world better? [Y/N]

- Is it worth five years (or more) of your time? [Y/N]

- Would you like to be known for this? [Y/N]

- Can you align your various capabilities with this opportunity? [Y/N]

You want to answer *yes* to all four questions before moving forward. Determining your personal mission is kind of a funneling process, where you start broad and then tighten your focus as your overall dreams and ideals become clear.

~~~

Push and Pull

In addition to providing you with clarity, a personal mission allows you to attract the right people and opportunities, and catalyzes other great opportunities that stem from your work, often unexpectedly. Especially during the first five years of your career, you will likely be seeking opportunities that you can fit into. I define this approach of fitting in as a push strategy. Pushing can yield quick results and short-term satisfaction, and I would say most people's careers fall into this bucket. It involves searching for job listings online, reaching out to companies you're interested in, submitting applications, and taking the promotion or the next job that comes around (probably without having insight as to your big picture).

The focus of the push strategy is to proactively seek out job opportunities and make yourself visible to potential employers. It's also about looking one or two jobs ahead for the next opportunity down the road. You spend time upskilling for what is needed for your next career advancement, and you may hop around a bit to gain the experience and compensation you desire. Although pushing is the way most people start their careers and a great career can work by pushing from one job to the next, it will require a lot of luck to achieve anything close to your desired personal mission.

In contrast, a pull strategy leans heavily upon self-knowledge, deep expertise, and being focused on your personal impact. When you can communicate your mission clearly, the right opportunities come to you. You magnetize people and situations, and your path takes you in unique directions. It pulls you forward. You acquire special and unusual qualifications, which means you end up with more than just job security. You end up being in demand for the opportunities you value.

If you can inspire people, you pull them along on your personal mission. Debbie Sterling's path to success wasn't paved with venture capital or massive resources. She launched GoldieBlox through a Kickstarter campaign and leveraged social media to create viral content, strategically building a network of supporters and collaborators.

Interestingly, Debbie's grandmother, who she never met, was an animator in Hollywood during the 1950s—a trailblazing role model in her own family. Through her family stories, Debbie learned about her grandmother's accomplishments and recognizes her own creative talents as possibly stemming from her. Subconsciously following in her grandmother's footsteps, Debbie is now largely focused on creating animated characters to introduce girls to STEM.

Debbie Sterling's story is a powerful reminder that our contributions to the world often originate from our unique experiences, perspectives, and passions. By staying true to her personal mission and leveraging her distinctive capabilities, Debbie has not only built a successful company but has also made significant strides in addressing the gender gap in STEM fields. Her journey exemplifies how aligning our work with our values and experiences can lead to both personal fulfillment and meaningful societal impact.

The pull approach very much relies upon a calling, and focusing on what you want to contribute to the world. Your career hours are focused on your valuable contribution, and you are usually not competing directly with anyone else. Your network is uniquely focused on where you are going, and you build a compelling reputation in your field of interest. Two of my all-time heroes are (were) just like this: Jane Goodall and Nelson Mandela. But aside from these well-known examples, all the people I have interviewed for this book have carved out their own niches, too. And you can as well.

In the pull position, you are equally interviewing any company or partner that you do business with. It's the power of passion and conviction. It's the uncommon expertise that evolves when you know that you are on this earth to do great things and make your career *worthwhile*. The job ahead needs to be worth *your* time.

A pull strategy is less opportunistic and may require more planning and patience, but it can lead to achieving the most audacious plan for yourself. Realistically, any long career will include both, and a push strategy can easily morph into a pull strategy once you get established in your field.

Something That Excites You

To enjoy the Upward Spiral, your work needs to feel enjoyable (maybe not all the time, but at least a good portion of the time). I'm not advocating to sacrifice your personal dreams for the common good. Instead, you can harness those dreams and make them real *while* working toward the greater good. Having a clear direction allows you to consciously and creatively weave in your desired contribution along the way.

Maybe you dream of becoming a jewelry designer. Great! You can still make your life's work a contribution to the whole by choosing to use only ethically mined materials, such as Pippa Small Jewelry in the UK. Known for her beautiful, ethically made jewelry that celebrates local artisans and communities, Pippa is an ambassador of the human rights organization Survival International and has won numerous awards for social responsibility.[5] Or maybe you hire and train disadvantaged workers, and educate consumers by designing pieces that have ecological themes.

Maybe you want to be a professional athlete like Sadio Mané, a Senegalese professional soccer star who plays as a forward for Bundesliga Bayern Munich and the Senegal national team. His main goals as a high-profile athlete are not to revel in the fame and fortune that he has achieved; instead, he contributes part of his wealth to the well-being and improvement of his original hometown, Bambali. For example, he financed the construction of a £455,000 public hospital in his village including a maternity care unit.[6]

Although he has achieved his athletic dreams playing professional soccer, Mané remains deeply connected to and motivated by improving life for people in his hometown community.

Finding and doing whatever excites you—even it if doesn't obviously or directly involve a worldwide problem—can be done while making a positive change in the world. This is because problems also present opportunities.

Global issues are too big for any one person. You don't have to solve all the problems in your community or the world alone or in your lifetime, just advance something you care about deeply. There are so many incredible ways to get involved in positive change, working in different capacities without self-sacrifice.

YOUR NEXT BIG MOVER

As you reflect on the insights and exercises from this chapter, consider the following: What is one powerful leap you can take to move your uniquely designed personal mission forward? What Big Mover action could propel you closer to maximizing your contribution in service of creating a positive impact?

Take a moment to capture your Big Mover in your workbook or the following.

_____

_____

_____

_____

CHAPTER 5

YOUR COMPENSATION

How would you like to be rewarded for your great work?

JUST LIKE GRACE, I NOTICE many mission-driven individuals struggling to balance their financial needs alongside their desires to contribute to solving our world's problems. Traditionally, work built around meaning offers lower financial compensation (including not-for-profit roles, social impact jobs, government roles, education, and healthcare support). Different from generations ago, young, ambitious workers have access to an abundance of information on jobs available and salaries through online sources ranging from TikTok to Glassdoor, and therefore, they are well aware of their opportunity costs when it comes to their work.

Several years back, a company called PayScale conducted research to track the difference between not-for-profit and for-profit jobs with the same job title, and their results showed pay decreases for not-for-profit jobs anywhere from 4% to 18%.[1] Adding to this gap are certain higher-paying jobs that tempt the most financially driven students right out of university or graduate school that don't have not-for-profit equivalent titles to compare, such as management consulting or investment banking. It is certainly difficult to compete to hire under this pay discrepancy reality. However, driven by a deep interest to contribute positively to their community or topic of interest, people like Grace continue to fill those roles that keep our societies functioning. But here's the issue: when the cost-benefit ratio is out of balance, the workers eventually leave the sector, or they burn out over time.

For many of these meaningful jobs, there is an unspoken ask on the people they hire that may sound familiar: "Ask not what your company can do for you—ask what you can do for your company." Alongside that ask, there is limited formal recognition, honor, or medals for personally shouldering the deficit for the greater good.

Not-for-profits historically have been designed to meet the needs of underrepresented people and programs that governments or the private sector do not address sufficiently. These organizations are often underfunded and rely on grants and donations, although this is partially changing with earned income models and generous philanthropy. Many young people entering the not-for-profit sector will cycle out of it after their first few years, mostly due to the lack of compensation and upward mobility (with limited or no retirement savings, senior employees hold on to their jobs when they are reliant on that income to live). What makes this pay issue thornier is that the people who take on these roles are either able to generously volunteer their time (they don't require monetary compensation since they have other financial resources) or they are part of the community the organization serves (often low-income or underrepresented groups); however, the low-salary sacrifice perpetuates their own poverty.

Yes, we need more workers in these essential roles who will accept the trade-offs. However, I am here to represent workers like Grace, who don't want to trade compensation for contribution; they want both. Many do-gooders are in constant internal negotiations between the reward from their impact and the allure of financial stability. Girls, especially, are brought up receiving high-fives for putting their community first or "always thinking of others." This type of good-girl conditioning sets young women up to overlook their own needs in service of others. But there is a personal price that they pay for that, including their health, income, and influence, and that's what Grace is realizing now.

The teaching profession is a well-known example of the struggle for compensation versus contribution. In the US, our teachers face an uphill struggle every day and were especially challenged during the COVID-19 pandemic. Although this role is vital, teachers receive financial compensation far below the societal value they provide. These workers struggle between their desire to make a difference and the external structures that undervalue their contributions, resulting in burnout. They hardly make ends meet while struggling to keep safe and shape the future leaders of their communities.

But unfortunately, that imbalance also keeps many people from choosing those fields in the first place. Understandably, income is a key part of most workers' motivation and reward. The number of open teaching positions in the US reveals our education system's inability to attract talent—and our seeming unwillingness to make this valuable work financially attractive. In January 2023, the data collected by the Annenberg Institute at Brown University showed 36,000 teacher vacancies in the US and another 163,000 teachers employed but not qualified to meet the requirements for the job. To attract the necessary talent, enhancing how teachers are compensated is a critical consideration. Already, some efforts have been made to fill in the hiring gaps, including offering student loan forgiveness, helping with mortgages, and switching schools to four-day weeks. However, until the compensation feels worth it for the ever-expanding roles of our teachers, these jobs will sit empty.[2]

We should also think more broadly than income when it comes to compensation. For example, some teachers do feel satisfied with the balance of their work. They may draw significant satisfaction from working with children, having summers free, and filling this essential role. This is an important point: we are each responsible for determining what compensation is worth our while, and there is no one size fits all.

However, in education, looking at the macro view of the number of job openings in education indicates that most teachers are not finding their balance: the reward they receive is not worth what they give. When these megatrends become obvious and impossible to ignore, change eventually happens. Meanwhile, students are suffering the consequences, and Band-Aid solutions such as a four-day workweek to entice teachers ultimately cost the students in the end. Looking at the teaching profession is just one example that helps highlight the needs of the perceived value of the compensation to at least match the perceived effort put into the job.

For Grace, taking a deeper look at her compensation desires is critical. Is she receiving too little for her hard work? Or is she being compensated in other ways that she is overlooking? By not paying tribute to some of her noneconomic compensation, she may later regret a change that leads to more money but less overall satisfaction. For people like Grace who are afraid of disappointing others, the idea of charging more for their valuable work seems incongruent with the end customers they are serving. They have been trained to be in service of something greater even if it's at their own expense. In simple terms, you give energy to your contribution to the world, and for doing so, you receive energy back from your work in some form. It's a cycle of to and from. To be satisfied, Grace—and the rest of us—need to balance that exchange so that we are not sending out more energy than we are receiving. See the following simplified drawing.

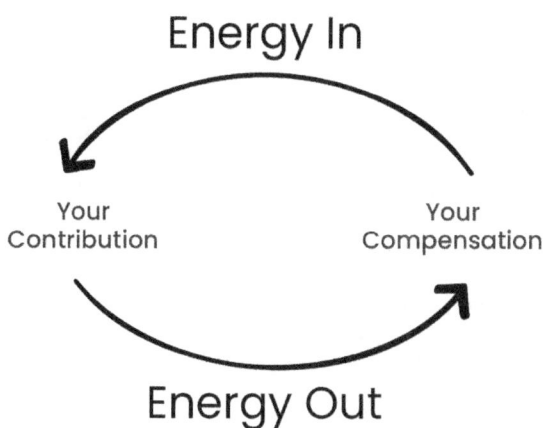

Energy In

Your Contribution

Your Compensation

Energy Out

Figure 5.1. Compensation Energy Diagram

When Grace and I first began working together, she wanted to act quickly on her desire for more financial stability. She was already considering a jump into investment banking or venture capital, purely for increased income. From firsthand experience, I know it's harder to convince the Uninspired Achiever to consider focusing on their contribution to the world, especially once their lifestyles demand they keep up the pace, than keeping an Unrewarded Do-Gooder like Grace in the game. However, the Graces of the world should not have to shoulder the burden of income deficit either. And this is the exciting part that feeds both my own contribution and compensation: helping people navigate over to the Well-Rewarded Disruptor.

We lose in a myriad of ways when people doing the most valuable jobs in our communities are not rewarded sufficiently. We know that our current system of capitalism and government undervalues many of the most vital roles in our communities. But that's not going to change overnight, and we don't have time to wait. If enough people like Grace pass on carrying the deficit burden, eventually our private and public sector leaders will notice and, hopefully, step in.

> We lose in a myriad of ways
> when people doing the most
> valuable jobs in our communities
> are not rewarded sufficiently.

Worthy Compensation

So far, we have mostly looked at the external factors holding Grace from her ideal balance. But there are internal factors too, such as false myths and unnecessary narratives that we hold as truths, often influenced by our culture. Shifting our mindsets to be able to take advantage of and grow the emerging opportunities where both income and meaning are growing fast is our next step.

For example, the either-or scenario of doing well or doing good is a false dichotomy. There is a rapidly growing sector of jobs that allows for both. The companies you are reading about in this book fit that category. Along with some obvious categories such as education (especially EdTech), healthcare and wellness, finance, and green technology/renewable energy, having it all is available to you.

A second limiting belief is that if you want an impactful career, you shouldn't "sell out" to a for-profit company. For-profit and not-for-profit are tax structures. If you care about impact, look for opportunities where you can make one regardless of its tax advantage. In some cases, a not-for-profit model is the best way to grow, build trust, and deliver results. Khan Academy, an educational organization, has an earned income not-for-profit model so that they are paid by schools that can offer accounts to their students (in addition to raising significant grants). But in other cases, like Virta Health, the model needs to be for-profit to broaden its reach. And the good that the company generates is as significant as the money they have raised (a lot!).

The idea that to positively impact our world, you can only work in the not-for-profit sector is antiquated. Handfuls of my past clients have felt committed to working in the not-for-profit world upon graduation. Anything else, in their words, makes them a sell-out, and that's also how they judge their classmates who are not following their same path.

Today, many emerging for-profit businesses are tackling societal and planetary needs. They are businesses with clear missions and well-defined values. Their for-profit structure allows them to raise money, take on investors, hire top talent, and spend money to gain market share. So naturally, they can afford higher salaries and compensate their employees more generously.

I'm not saying our society needs to move away from not-for-profits by any means. In many cases, they are the only model that can allow for the transparency or trust needed to tackle a particular problem. Instead, individually, you should focus on the contribution you want to deliver and the compensation you want to receive in return, then find the best way to achieve both. The legal structure of the organization has little to do with your contribution to its cause.

Third, you are worthy of a salary that feels worth your contribution! Many do-gooders need to shift their mindset to become open to receiving good compensation for their work. That means acknowledging and welcoming your desires, jealousy, and resentment. These emotions can feel particularly uncomfortable and out of character for the do-gooder, but they are a symptom of your imbalance. Jealousy that your friends can afford a new car or an apartment may feel uncomfortable, but before you beat yourself up for having that thought, what is it telling you? Hint: you want more.

Learning to accept that you can receive a fair income for your impact is an important step in opening yourself up to the right balance of compensation and contribution. As you already know, if you lean too far to the side of compensation, you may feel directionless and robotic, but if you lean too far into your contribution, you may suffer financially for it. You need both; we all do. This balance is critical for two main reasons: I want you to build a career that's *worth it* doing amazing and meaningful work, and you can't do your best work when your needs are barely being met. In fact, the more the do-gooders prosper, the more capacity they have to contribute, amplifying their positive influence.

Some people think that because you can feel it, you are responsible for what's not fair in the world. Nope. Most likely you did not create the problems. But you do get to choose to be responsible and use your sensitivity to contribute to the world positively, but only in ways that work for you too.

Finally, it's a fiction that the perfect job exists. Work is work. There will be aspects that feel overwhelming or remedial and other parts that light you up. You are compensated for all of these tasks. The key is to be intentional about what you want to gain from your current situation and to make sure it delivers on that. Likely, at some point, you will need to grow further, and that's when you need a shift to a new position or to a new company (or perhaps it's time to start your own venture).

Our financial prosperity is tied to the positive transformations we catalyze. Ideally, you and Grace will be among the do-gooders who prosper. Money in the hands of good people is a great thing. If we can elevate people like Grace to positions of influence, where they are rewarded sufficiently, including financially, they are likely to also recirculate that money in more positive ways. Plus having them in a position of significant influence, such as a CEO, allows their values to shape our communities. When we get money and power into the hands of kind people, they vote with their time and wallets for good.

None of the people interviewed in this book started their projects and companies with making money as their primary goal, but they all had or developed a healthy relationship with money. They understood its usefulness as a tool for influence and change, and it creates opportunities. They appreciated money for what it could do for their work, for others, and for themselves personally. The higher they reached, the harder they worked, the more they believed in their creations, and the more money flowed to them in support of their endeavors.

Patagonia, the much beloved American retailer of outdoor recreation clothing, is the poster child of a for-profit company being overtly mission-driven. And they have already been a successful retail brand for over 50 years. They are a B-Corp, a for-profit company that has received certification as a company that meets certain social and environmental standards. From their website, you can easily read their core values, which are integrity, environmentalism, justice, and not being bound by convention. They are not only committed to creating exceptional, long-lasting products but also creating a catalyst for positive environmental change. The main reason they are in business is to protect our home planet.

And they mean it: "If we have any hope of a thriving planet—much less a business—it is going to take all of us doing what we can with the resources we have," said Yvon Chouinard, founder of Patagonia. In fact, from their new ownership structure, this is how committed they are: "Here's how it works: 100% of the company's voting stock transfers to the Patagonia Purpose Trust, created to protect the company's values, and 100% of the nonvoting stock has been given to the Holdfast Collective, a nonprofit dedicated to fighting the environmental crisis and defending nature. The funding will come from Patagonia: each year, the money we make after reinvesting in the business will be distributed as a dividend to help fight the crisis."[3]

If you love the outdoors, want a very inclusive work community, and have any experience in retail, Patagonia may have the right compensation for you. Retail itself is not as lucrative as other sectors, but because Patagonia is a steady business and a for-profit organization, they can pay a market wage for their employees, along with meaningful benefits. To sweeten the deal for the right-minded employee, they get to feel great about the contribution the company is making environmentally and socially. But again, what's right for one person is not the solution for the next, so keep working on your muscle that assesses the right balance for you.

In contrast, let's look at a US venture capital firm called Fifth Wall. In the past, they focused on property technology investment but have more recently shifted to climate tech. On their website, they point out that "real estate is the largest contributor to climate change, consuming 40% of the world's energy and producing 30%–40% of all greenhouse gas emissions. Yet historically, the industry has put very little capital toward technology solutions to mitigate its contributions." And they note that an investment of "$18 trillion is required over the next decade to get the real estate industry to net zero" emissions. They believe that their prior real estate knowledge positions them well to invest in companies that can contribute to this net-zero goal, and that is not only their "ethical imperative" but also the "economic opportunity of our lifetime."[4] Although Fifth Wall has a small employee base (only around 60 employees), they also invest in companies that also hire talent in the climate tech space. For example, one of their investments is a company called Loop, whose goal it is "to become a global leader in the electrification of transportation by bringing to market a suite of smart, simple, and affordable electric vehicle charging infrastructure solutions," enhancing the transition to electric vehicles.[5]

In June 2022, Business Wire reported that Fifth Wall announced the $500 million close of its inaugural climate fund. Jobs in private equity are not easy to break into.[6] For an associate venture capitalist role, hard skills such as financial modeling are required (lots of Excel), alongside soft skills such as networking (willingness to make calls and network). They often draw upon hiring investment bankers or management consultants who are used to long work hours and high expectations. This is a noteworthy reminder to think of a longer game when thinking about your career. Some career opportunities that may not be impact-driven are great stepping stones to the ones that are; that's why you are the one determining your definition of *good*. The compensation for venture capital roles tends to be compelling, but in addition, working alongside intelligent people investing to help an industry reach net zero emissions is part of that reward.

We have been trained as a society to judge money, and in the realm of doing good, it can be perceived as bad or wrong. It is not. It is a highly effective tool that, when wielded correctly, can do immeasurable good. Keep that in mind. Remember that if you make a lot of money doing good for the world, you've earned it. I'll say it again: money in the hands of good people is a very good thing.

Balance in Context

If you are like Grace and are struggling to see a solution for your compensation deficit, let's look at some pathways others have taken. As you are noticing, solving for compensation differences can take a variety of forms. Following are some examples that I have seen where the worker did not have to abandon their personal contribution to reach their own compensation goals.

A current educator, who loves working with young students, has a role as a belonging and inclusion specialist in a middle school. She uses part of her summers to do private-sector consulting on diversity, equity, and inclusion (DEI). She was able to build a side business as a DEI consultant, doing workshops, and used her teacher's training to develop her own coursework for her consulting role that applied to adults instead of children. It requires more of her time; however, she likes the change of scene from children to adults, and she feels good about being in control of her alternative income stream. Each role contributes toward her expertise in the area, which is a positive for job security too.

A junior program manager in the not-for-profit sector building awareness of factory farming switched jobs to a for-profit company that focuses on regenerative farming. Instead of spending her time exposing our race-to-the-bottom factory farming for maximum profit, she now works in a positive work environment that is solutions-based, which takes less from her emotionally. There are also many job opportunities emerging for her longer term on this path.

A high school math teacher switched to a not-for-profit EdTech company with an earned income business model (instead of solely relying on donations, which allows them to offer more income compensation to employees). He has been able to leverage his capabilities better in this environment than in the classroom, leaning into strengths such as statistics and financial modeling. In addition, he is now able to better support his growing family on his income.

A lawyer with deep expertise in sustainability decided to move to a city where the cost of living was less since he was able to work remotely. This meant he could earn a New York City lawyer hourly wage but live in the Midwest, where the income went way further. He loves his work and was happy to shift locations rather than careers. Also, in his new location, his tiny apartment was traded for a standalone house, he can afford vacations, and in general, he is living a more balanced life.

An engineer working in Silicon Valley wanted more meaning in her job. She is also conflicted since she is learning so much and gaining skills and expertise that set her up well for the future. Although her company is not mission-minded, they are great at supporting women engineers, and she is riding that wave. To feel comfortable spending a few more years in her current job, she decided to volunteer her extra time as a student mentor at a charitable start-up called Develop for Good, which connects computer scientist students with not-for-profits that need assistance.[7] This balance feels right for her for now, and it's broadening her network.

Exercise: What Is Worthy Compensation for You?

Because your own desired compensation is broader than salary alone, because it's subjective, and because it is emotionally charged, using a boilerplate approach will ensure that almost no one is satisfied. Think beyond traditional compensation elements to individualize rewards and make them meaningful. How you are compensated fairly for your work may be totally different from how the next person is compensated, even if you have the same job and salary.

Almost always, your total compensation includes monetary compensation. But anything that returns energy or value to you is compensation. That could mean the chance to work with someone extraordinary. For example, if you are a chimpanzee biologist or a conservationist, working alongside Jane Goodall may mean you would be willing to earn less income due to her star power. Your current job could be a chance to greatly expand your network or switch to a different field of interest or develop a skillset you want. It might mean working the hours that you need or the flexibility to work from a rainforest in Costa Rica. Feeling proud of your work also gives you energy. Curiously understanding your compensation needs from an energy-in standpoint is crucial to finding that balance.

Start by marking a circle along the following line. How satisfied are you with your compensation? A response at the far left means you are entirely unsatisfied, and a circle on the far right means you are completely satisfied. These following exercises for compensation will take you 30 to 45 minutes to complete.

Now do the same exercise again, but this time mark an X on the same lines for where you want to be in two years.

Example: Grace's compensation

0 ——————— O ——————— X ——————————————— 10

Your compensation

0 ———————————————————————————————— 10

What does this tell you about your compensation? What is the main reason driving the gap (if any)?

———————————————————————————————————

———————————————————————————————————

———————————————————————————————————

———————————————————————————————————

Now let's get to specifics. In your current role, what compensation do you receive? For example, list the tangible inputs such as salary, bonus, or healthcare.

———————————————————————————————————

———————————————————————————————————

———————————————————————————————————

———————————————————————————————————

Now think more broadly. What are the less obvious factors contributing to your job (giving you energy to keep working hard)? For example, is it the people you have access to for building your network? Or the city you get to live in which is close to your family? The alignment of the mission? The expertise you are gaining? Or chance to work remotely? List everything you can think of.

_____

_____

_____

_____

_____

Next, let's go back to the initial scale. After doing this exercise, do the places of the circle and X move at all? Some people realize they are actually getting more nonmonetary compensation than they were giving their job credit for.

Let's see if there are any minimum compensation requirements for you to meet in the next six months and two years.

_____

_____

_____

_____

_____

_____

What will these changes afford you?

_____

_____

_____

_____

What are some possible pathways you can research that may get you there?

_____

_____

_____

_____

What myth do you need to let go to move yourself forward?

_____

_____

Finally, what is your biggest takeaway regarding compensation?

_____

_____

_____

For the work you are contributing to the world, it is important that you are conscious about receiving for your giving. People often think of compensation in terms of income earned. What I have found in working with clients and feeling inspired with their work over a long term is that their rewards are well beyond the financial gain. Everybody assesses these rewards differently, and they change depending on your stage in life and the responsibilities you hold and the desires you have.

For me, I go back to the energy in and out diagram at the beginning of this chapter. It has taken me a long time to take note of the ingredients that give me energy. It's always been easier to understand what takes my energy. You can only rise up the Upward Spiral if you are able to receive in return for your giving. The trick is to think more broadly about what you are receiving than we are culturally taught to do. The appropriate rewards will help you stay motivated over many years.

~~~~~~

What If You Are Not Compensated Sufficiently?

When going through this exercise, Grace noted that she is looking for a minimum salary of $85,000 in the next two years to allow her to start saving. As she suspected, her current role at her foundation is not sustainable in that regard, and she needs to pursue an alternative. She also noted that she has gained so much from this early part of her career. She listed "confidence" as one of her alternative compensation attributes, along with "developed clear values" and "built a strong network of contributors." She also realized that part of her current dissatisfaction stemmed from her having already gained those benefits, and therefore, they hold less weight in her situation today. Knowing that she wanted to earn more salary helped her imagine what that salary could afford her; things like "a trip with her parents" and "the option to start a family in the future" were on that list. And she felt excited to have those options. She is also aware that she wants to focus on refining her personal mission and to see how she can combine all those needs, letting go of her false understanding of for-profit companies.

Without doing this exploratory work, she may have made a rushed decision to abandon her do-gooder role and switch to the Uninspired Achiever to avoid the burnout she is experiencing. In this quadrant, she will likely receive significantly higher compensation, but she may be forced to give up alignment with her values and contribution desires. Although this route may offer relief in the short term, knowing Grace and her desire to do great things in the world, it will be a temporary fix.

I have also noticed that graduate school surfaces as an option with people who are undercompensated and unhappy with their career trajectory. For various reasons, sometimes they do not do any exploratory work on what the compensation, including salaries, will be on the other side of their additional degree. They can find themselves in the same financial situation with even more student debt a few years later. Before saying yes to more education, look ahead to what will open up for you and whether those opportunities will meet your total compensation needs.

Contrary to Grace, I have also worked with and know many individuals who have chosen financially attractive work opportunities, abandoning any responsibility to contribute back to the world. The regret in their stories is deep, but they are often unable to exit their chosen path because now their lifestyles require a significant income, and the switching costs later in a career are much more challenging. So they carry that regret in their career and personal lives.

What if we can help Grace's career trajectory by introducing her to opportunities where she can continue her impactful work and also be compensated fairly, becoming a Well-Rewarded Disruptor instead? In this quadrant, her well-being is considered, and she can continue to develop and pursue her passions leaving her mark on the world.

For lots of young professionals, understanding the costs associated with their desired lifestyle is a necessary piece of research that is easy to access. Research the cost of living in the city you live in or want to live in, then for any job pathways you may be considering, research the salary range. Given your current expertise, note where you will likely fall on that range. You can search LinkedIn for people who have had those roles, and then see what came after for them. Know the average salaries for those roles too, so you can understand the trajectory.

Especially if you are a valuable employee, being open and discussing your needs with your manager or company mentor can help set you up for the success you desire. Communicate your needs, but don't feel you need to justify or overexplain anything. I have witnessed many people shifting roles within a company to better meet their compensation desires. It's amazing what a well-thought-out "ask" will open for you. In addition, a good manager will want to see you grow, and they may also have resources for you to consider within the broader network. Perhaps a supplier to your current company? Or a consulting firm helping on specific projects? Your ask doesn't have to be threatening; instead, it's an opportunity for them to understand what you are looking for longer term, and to see if they can be a partner to help you think about the next steps.

Identifying your ideal role or company outside your current employer is next. If salary were not a short-term concern, we could add to this by looking into starting a business that leverages your existing capabilities. Perhaps you've noticed a void in the supply chain. Grace is looking for financial security right now, so entrepreneurship is not the best option for her. Especially when unemployment is low, it's a great time to leverage your advantage and make a switch within your existing company, or in another. If you meet 70% of the job description, apply to open roles. But also remember that your best asset is to leverage your existing network.

For any new job, make sure you spend time understanding the expected broader compensation there too. You can gather a great list of questions to ask, given what you already know about your capabilities, your contribution, and your desired compensation.

Finding the Balance

Ntefeleng Nene was raised by two teachers and currently works at a global not-for-profit called The Bridgespan Group from their South African office. Bridgespan is a company focused on building a better world by strengthening the ability of mission-driven organizations and philanthropists to achieve breakthrough results in addressing society's most important challenges and opportunities. Like many of us, when Ntefeleng was graduating from high school, she was unsure of her work prospects. She was from a rural area in South Africa, and there was no career guidance at her school at all. She sat down with her father to discuss her next steps, and she told him she did not know what she wanted to do with her career. All she had been exposed to was the teaching profession (through the lens of her parents), and she was not interested in pursuing that.[8]

She remembers saying as a 17-year-old, "I really want to do work that will allow me to help people." And her father then said, "Okay, if that's what you want to do, maybe you can do social work."

Without knowing much about her prospects, she decided to move forward with that suggestion and go to university to study social work. Only once she was close to graduation and looking for employment did she understand the huge financial limitations of a career in social work: "I had such a rude awakening in terms of the salary of a social worker." Looking back, she noted that was her first deep career reflection moment.

Somehow, the universe had other plans for Ntefeleng, and with some guidance, she went straight into studying public health and got her master's in public health law. "A friend of mine said, 'There's this interesting program. It's new in the university. Let's do it.'" And so she did, still without considering her longer-term plans or desires.

In parallel with pursuing her master's, she found herself working as a clinical social worker. The work was deeply meaningful, but it was very difficult emotionally, and her job was not sustainable, given how drained she felt. Her second reflection moment came as soon as she started her job. The orphan babies of parents who had died of HIV/AIDS were being dropped off at her organization, needing to be cared for. Taking care of these children was not in the job description, but it became the reality of her role, along with finding these children new families and homes to grow up in through foster care and adoption.

Ntefeleng vulnerably shared with me, "My heart was just not strong enough to deal with or to carry what I had to do at that time." She was too close to the pain and suffering of the people she wanted to help. At this point, she realized she needed to rethink how she could fulfill her dream to help people in need. She loved that each day she could directly feel that she was making a difference, but the emotional weight of her job was costing her too much personally. She was putting in all the energy she had, but it was not coming back to her in equal amounts.

Her solution was to move to community development. Her logic was that "it might take longer to actually see the results, and I might not feel the change directly, but maybe I can still help." She went into facilitating support groups for people living with HIV, which was still emotionally taxing work but felt more manageable for her energetically. "And that's where I actually started working with NGOs [nongovernmental organizations], got to understand the donor landscape, like what does it mean for an organization to be funded?"

However, after working hard in this community development role, her low compensation gradually wore on her. Frustrated, she didn't see a financial way out, given the dire need for resources, and she was being squeezed personally. "The donor gives you $100 and out of the hundred, $99 needs to go to the program. I get it." But her unmet needs were taking their toll on her energy levels, and she was tired. She was working so hard to help others but was unable to help herself. "What about my bonus? What about my livelihood? What about my family? I also need income. And I didn't have answers to any of that." But she was fully aware of her struggle, and she wanted more for herself and her family.

Once you are conscious of your situation, the opportunities that you desire show up. After working with different NGOs, one Saturday at a social gathering, Ntefeleng randomly spoke with a person from a global for-profit consulting firm. She admitted she did not have consulting experience, but the for-profit consulting firm was interested in her deep sector knowledge and health-related network, and they were willing to teach her how to be a consultant. So she switched gears again—significantly this time.

The new position meant that she now had more financial security, but the work was not necessarily aligned with her impact interests or her values. There was a social impact business within the firm, and so she soon pursued that pathway, where she hoped for the best of all worlds. She lucked out, and the new position was another step toward balancing both of her compensation needs and contribution desires. For the first time, she loved her work and the impact she was able to achieve. She was closer to having the right balance of give and receive, and she felt enthusiastic and energized by her work.

She now was used to the consulting salary, so no matter what interesting opportunity crossed her path those days, returning to a development work salary for significantly less was off the table. But although she loved her impact work, she knew she had even more to give beyond what she could do in this for-profit consulting firm environment. "And out of the blue, somebody on LinkedIn reached out. They said, 'Listen, there's this organization [The Bridgespan Group]. They are setting up in Africa. Would you be interested?'"

Through her interviews with The Bridgespan Group, she understood even more her work needs and interests. "I need to go back to my core values of driving impact. But I need someone who's going to pay what it's worth," and the rest is history. "I really was looking for that kind of environment that will not make me compromise.

"When I joined Bridgespan, I wanted to contribute to Africa owning its own development agenda. And I asked myself, 'What does that look like? How can that happen? What is it that I need to do on a daily basis to drive that ambition of seeing Africa owning its development agenda instead of being influenced by the global north?'"

After she homed in on the impact she desired to make in her career, her new role working with Bridgespan clients led her to work very closely with philanthropies, advising them on African development issues and needs, guiding them in the appropriate directions so their economic contributions made the most difference where it most counted.

Ntefeleng's story weaves in her journey to find the right balance. When I interviewed her for this book, she was energized and very content with her job. Her journey had involved some twists and turns, and some extra student fees, but they also helped her to land in the spot where she is now. She had found a place that could challenge her in the right way, and where she could meet her own need too.

Be Open to More

No doubt it can be more challenging to look for more generous opportunities that don't compromise your values or goals. But this mindset shift is a personal choice. We need to decide that we want to reach our potential. We need to open ourselves up to receiving more. Most of the people I have coached embrace the concept, and they feel free and energized by the switch. But actually embracing and living in a different way takes time.

Beginning to notice where your self-talk or society normalizes accepting less than you contribute is the first step. And then taking time to imagine and reflect on the possibilities of the alternative that comes next. You will know that you have embraced what's needed when you notice opportunities to prosper are everywhere. Surround yourself with people who embody being rewarded for their efforts and can encourage you to recognize your worth. Use your imagination to visualize the life you want, taking out the "should" and other limiting do-gooder self-talk. Insisting on adequate compensation is not selfish; it's for everyone's benefit.

This mindset shift can be a gradual process, and with intention and patience, you can cultivate a world where you can receive more for your hard and valuable work. Can you commit to this? Once you believe you are worthy of fair compensation, and you can visualize yourself working hard and being rewarded abundantly, the world mysteriously presents you with new opportunities offering you just that. They probably have been there all along, but you are now aware and can recognize them and take action when they come your way. This allows you to not only do the work you love but to also value it appropriately. What feels abundant and energizing for you may be different from others, so stay away from comparison and judgment. Instead, work on creating for yourself a reward system that replenishes you after your hard work so that you can keep going.

A healthy relationship with power and money is an important element to consider if you have the ambition to do fantastic work for good in our world. When you pursue your dreams with dedication and align your actions with your larger vision, financial success tends to follow naturally as a result of your aligned efforts. By prioritizing your impact and the positive change you can bring, you create the conditions for both personal fulfillment and financial abundance to show up.

YOUR NEXT BIG MOVER

As you reflect on the insights and exercises from this chapter, consider the following: What is one powerful step you can take to receive the right compensation? What Big Mover action could propel you closer to feeling sufficiently rewarded for your great work?

Take a moment to capture your Big Mover in your workbook or the following.

_____

_____

_____

_____

CHAPTER 6

YOUR CONNECTIONS

How will you nurture your
relationships to support
your valuable work?

THERE IS NO GOING IT alone when it comes to your career, and
you cannot reach the Upward Spiral for Good on your own. The
people you weave into your daily work expand what's possible for
you. An authentic connection with yourself and with the people
around you will shape who you become and what you can contribute. For you to realize your personal mission, the people in your life
will offer you two critical components for your success.

The first is a safety net. This determines how soft your landing
will be when you fall, fail, or need some support to keep going.
Your safety net is typically made up of your inner circle of closest
influences. The second is more like a trampoline; when your career

bounces upward, they can launch you higher. These are the people who create opportunities for you. These are the connections that will leapfrog you over hurdles, obstacles, and hassles, and help you go further faster.

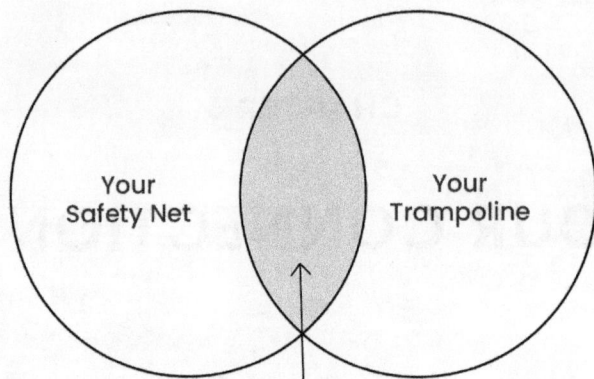

Some people may serve as both

Figure 6.1. Safety Net + Trampoline Diagram

Your Safety Net

Part of being human is our requirement of a deep connection to others. Your most treasured resource in your journey to positively impact our world will be your inner circle, and I have yet to find a case of a Well-Rewarded Disruptor who is void of such a support group. These people closest to you form your safety net, encouraging you, supporting you through struggles and cushioning your falls. Most career-oriented books or courses overlook the importance of this support system. If you ask a person who has realized great success professionally who helped them achieve their success, they will no doubt mention someone in this small sphere. That person is probably a family member or close friend. You may not be working with them in your career, but they offer the needed prod, cushion, or shoulder to lean on behind the scenes (and sometimes, the inspiration).

I had the chance to meet former Facebook data scientist Frances Haugen, known as the Facebook whistleblower who accused her employer of pursuing profit over safety. I asked her where she gathered the emotional strength to move ahead with her decision to come forward and expose Facebook's harmful business practices. She already had a clear view of right and wrong through her ethical lens, but taking on a unicorn start-up that grew into a worldwide behemoth is not easy by any means. Her answer was this: she moved home to live under her parents' roof to receive their love and care. Feeling safe at home and having a place to reflect, rest, and recharge gave her the courage to align with her values and do the right thing. She also was offered great support from other individuals and organizations; however, without the safety net of her parents, she could not have taken this brave step.[1]

To understand the importance of your inner circle, I like to borrow a philosophy from the Gottman Institute and apply it to your inner circle.[2] The institute's focus is on relationships, but they have a concept called the *emotional bank account*, which is relevant here too. We each have this invisible or intangible account, and we are either adding in emotional value, or taking it out through our daily interactions and experiences. Just like a financial bank account, there are withdrawals and deposits. To have the energy to tackle some of the world's big issues, your emotional bank account cannot be empty, let alone overdrawn.

At any given time, you either have a surplus, are neutral (at zero), or have a deficit of energy. The people in your inner circle are the ones you can count on to deposit into your account (and you theirs, hopefully), giving you a surplus.

Day-to-day life experiences, on the other hand, take emotional energy away from your account. Whether it's being told "no" to a job you wanted, being treated unkindly, or losing someone close to you, all those negative life experiences remove energy resources from your emotional bank account. The hope is that you can operate more often from a surplus than a deficit, and being conscious of this concept is a step toward that.

But it's more complicated than just an equal exchange of good and bad deposits. Unfortunately, the ability to deposit into your account is more cumbersome than it is to deplete it. The Gottman Institute, a mental health and relationships organization, uses a ratio for everyday life: "20 positive interactions to every one negative interaction." I'm not sure if we all have the same ratio, but I do know that we humans have a well-documented negativity bias, meaning we pay more attention to what's wrong than what's right. Regardless of the right ratio for you, your inner circle needs to be a lot more generous with authentic support than life depletes you. If you are on empty, you cannot be generous with your work.

Grace already has the quality relationships she needs for this safety net. However, for various reasons, she feels like she needs to do it all on her own. Showing vulnerability has not been something she learned growing up, and at work, the perception that she has it all under control has paid off in promotions. But as she takes on more responsibility in her work and personal life, she feels the weight of it all, and it keeps her up at night. And what she does not yet know is that if she can let down her guard with the people who care for her; they can help shoulder some of the stress she feels. But even more rewarding is that they then can also ask the same of her, which significantly deepens the connection for everyone. The idea that it's a privilege to be in someone's inner circle has not clicked for her, and currently, she does not want to "burden" anyone. This sentiment is not helpful for Grace's personal development, and it will begin to hold her back as the pressure mounts.

Who are the people in your inner circle? We know that we need human connection just like we need food and water. These deep, meaningful connections are a powerful force of emotional capital. For some, family naturally plays that role, be it a partner, a sibling, a parent, or an aunt. But it is by no means limited to family. It's more about how your inner circle shows up for you and holds space for you than anything else.

Your safety net is rooting for you on the sidelines and wants to watch you succeed. They celebrate when you have success and can also keep you company and offer support when you need to recharge or to be still. You can be vulnerable with them, and they won't use that against you. They will fight for you, listen to you, and beneath it all, they accept you. If there is an opportunity with your name on it, they will raise their hand for you, even if you are not in the room. They believe in your potential. These relationships are most likely not formally announced as "You're in my inner circle," but you know they will make time for you when you need them. Developing and nurturing those deep and meaningful relationships will dramatically enhance your life's potential.

This group may consist of a few to a handful of people. Although it's helpful to have multiple cheerleaders, more is not more. You need quality and authentic cheering, and everyone can develop these bonds. Your emotional bank account is filled when these people listen to your ideas and remind you what is unique and special about you. They support your efforts and shout your praises from the rooftops.

You, in Your Inner Circle?

Much of the work in this book requires you to look in the mirror and take stock of who you are, including your values and other capabilities, plus tuning into what you care about. The more honest and curious you can be with yourself, the closer you will get to the essence that makes you so valuable to the world. And you will feel more confident when you can show up knowing the value you can offer the world.

I have in the past been my biggest critic. And throughout that time, I also heard a small voice that could see something far more powerful and beautiful inside myself, buried deep below the doubt. I believe that we all have a glimpse, at least, of this inner cheerleader who can see something more for ourselves. If you are hearing those cheers in the distance, your work is to tune into it. Give that voice the main stage in your head theatrics. Turn the volume down on the critic. It is serving no one, except perhaps your competition. It's really a decision to embrace positive self-talk, awareness of when the negative voice creeps in, and then form the habit of redirecting the thought. You can change the voice; I have (mostly) done it. It's in your control to redirect your thoughts.

Given this, as strange as this may sound, you are only a candidate for your own safety net. That's right: you're not guaranteed admission into your valuable inner circle. You have to earn it. Being a positive contributor to your emotional bank account instead of a detractor is a critical and intentional decision.

From working with clients, I have noticed how often they are not on their own side. That overly critical voice sounds like "I am not good enough to do X" or "I am not qualified to X." It starts early in life too. I hear kids say things to themselves such as "I am the worst reader" or "I am a bad student," which is heartbreaking. If you repeat these words to yourself often enough, eventually the talk in your head becomes "truths" that you hold in your body. A moment of self-doubt or feeling bad about not getting a result is normal and part of being human, but beating yourself up continually is not helpful. And it's also harder to attract others to believe in you if you are not able to believe in yourself. Please don't deplete your own account. Recruit yourself to your inner circle as soon as possible, so you can begin contributing positively to your emotional bank account.

> ## Being a positive contributor to your emotional bank account instead of a detractor is a critical and intentional decision.

Exercise: Core Connection Check-In

Your inner circle: make a list of who is in your inner circle at the moment.

_____ _____ _____ _____

_____ _____ _____ _____

The inner circle of others: make a list of whose inner circle you may be in at the moment.

——————— ——————— ——————— ———————

——————— ——————— ——————— ———————

What are the changes, if any, you would like to see?

_____

_____

∼∼∼

The Trampoline

Your connection's other main role is to offer you a leg up, an opportunity to expand well beyond where you are today. Progress is not linear for many reasons, but your relationships have significant powers to advance you and your personal mission, leaping you significantly forward when the timing is right. If you are facing a major obstacle in your path, your trampoline can get you past it in ways you'd never imagine.

When your emotional bank account is replenished or you feel like you have the wind at your back, you are in an ideal place to push yourself further along your learning edge, especially when you feel brave. In these moments, it's time to tap into the various channels that can leap you ahead on your chosen path. Similar to your safety net, these connections can help you reach beyond what you imagined possible. However, different from the inner circle, these do not necessarily need to be close relationships, and sometimes they seem transactional. They are not equally or consistently valuable, but they can make all the difference when the ideal connection enters at the perfect time.

As mentioned earlier, Frances Haugen also had guardian angels looking after her interests as she publicly challenged the ethics of one of the world's most influential companies. For instance, she gained financial support from Omidyar Network (Pierre Omidyar, the eBay founder's philanthropic investment firm), which financed her lawyers aiding in the costs of taking on Facebook. This is a perfect example of a trampoline. You are not necessarily connected closely, but you are aligned, and together you can reach far greater heights.

Within and beyond your safety net and trampoline, your connections include everyone in your professional network ranging from your role models to your actual customers. All of these people form your network, your connection to the wider world that helps you succeed.

Your Professional Network

Your professional network is a critical resource to help you achieve your ambitious plans. Through your network, you will be connected to various resources, funding, expertise, information, best practices, and tools. It will help you tap into others who share your desire to contribute to topics that are meaningful to you both. Your network can help you multiply the impact that you bring to the world. Without a doubt, a strong network can help raise your profile, increasing your visibility and, ideally, awareness of the problems in the world you want to highlight and help solve. In tougher times, your network can shelter you, open the right door, or help you build resilience. It should also challenge you, especially with diverse perspectives and ideas that can lead to the most interesting solutions to solving complex problems. And when you need someone to sustain your efforts later in your career, your network will connect you with successors, partners, and supporters who can further grow your work.

The most widely used resource for communicating and maintaining your professional network is LinkedIn (but even if they are not connected to you through LinkedIn, those connections all have potential). If social platforms are not your thing, having a living resource where all your professional contacts are listed and where you are connected to their networks is not something you can bypass. Who you know really matters, and curating your network is a necessary investment. Far beyond networking for jobs, leveraging your connections will enhance your personal mission day to day. The following are several ways where your connections give you a considerable leg up.

Finding Shoulders to Stand On

Standing on the shoulders of successful people, whether you know them personally or have just read about them, helps you make progress faster. By learning from their experiences, you can leapfrog ahead, avoiding common mistakes and accelerating your own path to success.

There's plenty of wisdom to go around, but remember: it's a two-way street. Give credit to those who helped you along the way. Thank them and recognize their contributions. And when you've made it, be ready to help others up too. Don't miss out on the valuable insights you can gain from connecting with more experienced people.

As a new author, I've learned a lot by watching other nonfiction writers. It's been super helpful to see how they write and launch their books. I've paid special attention to authors who have a bigger purpose, using their books to spread important ideas or change how people think. By observing how these authors share their personal missions and connect with their readers, I've gotten a great head start. It's like I'm standing on their shoulders, even if it's just through their books or online presence. And when I've got more experience under my belt, I'm excited to pay it forward and help new authors too.

Exercise: On the Shoulders of Giants

Whose shoulders are you already standing on, and whose would you like to stand on to advance your personal mission?

_____ _____ _____ _____

_____ _____ _____ _____

How are you making it easy for others to stand on your shoulders?

_____

_____

_____

Meaningful Mentors

For an impactful career, mentorship is about enhancing your potential and wisdom, to further fuel your mission. It offers a boost of personal growth. Your mentors might offer advice, support, introductions, alternative viewpoints, encouragement, or just a sounding board. Some mentors can offer knowledge about your area of interest or industry trends and can help you navigate your professional path in your area of contribution. Other mentors are more personal and share an affinity or common background with you, which enables them to understand you and help you address the unique obstacles you may face. They can also serve as an accountability partner, build your confidence, and help you grow.

Jessica Lindl, general manager and vice president of social impact and education at Unity Technologies, had the following thoughts to share about engaging a mentor. "I would really focus on how they make you feel. I think that's overlooked. How supportive are they? Because their job is really to be championing you, not to be talking *at* you or showing how much they know. So number one is how do they make you feel? Two, are they going to actually provide you some insights into how you bring in your own social capital or use their social capital for you and what you're trying to achieve? Number three, really get clear what you're asking them to teach you and how you're hoping to benefit. People may get caught up a little bit more on the power of somebody and not really understand if what that person has to offer is related to their purpose and what they want to be going for."[3]

Most mentors are formed through warm leads—someone you know or once removed. But you can also be proactive and search LinkedIn for someone who might be a great fit for you. Search industry groups and professional organizations aligned with your interests. Connect and ask for recommendations. Once you've identified a potential mentor, reach out and introduce yourself. Tell them why you're approaching them and why you're interested in their field. Be professional and clear about what you hope to gain from the relationship and specific in your ask. Once you've established a mentorship relationship, use it. The more you put into the relationship, the more you will get out of it.

Listen to your mentors' advice when it is offered, but then apply it to your circumstance to see if it fits. No one knows what's best for you on all levels, and we are all on our own journey. Agree to this perspective before you start; some mentors take offense when their advice is not followed!

Exercise: Mentor Assessment

Who are your mentors and/or who would you like to be your mentors?

_____ _____ _____ _____

_____ _____ _____ _____

How are you mentoring others?

_____

_____

_____

Your Sphere of Influence

As you move deeper into your expertise and your career progresses over time, consider playing a leadership role in supporting your personal mission by bringing together different parts of the ecosystem that can catalyze your impact. Just like pieces of a puzzle coming together to build a picture, many successful Disruptors for Good can expand their impact by bringing the right people together to form a *sphere of influence*, connecting and rounding out the full ecosystem related to their personal mission. The pieces individually are worth more when they work together than when they are apart. In addition to increasing the impact of everyone involved, initiating a sphere of influence also adds to your personal credibility; you get to influence and drive the collective strategy, and you benefit financially (directly or indirectly).

Amy King is the founder and CEO of Pallet, a start-up that builds shelters for people experiencing homelessness, headquartered in Seattle. Her husband started a construction company that she eventually joined, and at one point, they learned that most of their workers had been recently released from prison, and many of them were homeless. These talented and hardworking people struggled to find work because of their legal and domestic situations, so Amy was inspired to start Pallet as a way to help these workers (who had become friends) by designing and manufacturing transitional shelters for displaced people. Through this work, her personal mission became clear, which is to end homelessness in her lifetime. The entire staff of Pallet, from the executive director and manager on down to the installation crews, was hired after their release from correctional institutions.[4]

Having done a short stint working for a nonprofit that ran out of grant money, Amy knew she wanted to stick with using a traditional for-profit structure for Pallet. "I kept thinking, 'How can you make something that helps people, but is also self-sustaining and not always dependent on grants, and philanthropy, and the goodwill of others?' I wanted to be able to help people and know I could count on always providing these services."

Initially, Pallet built a community containing 58 single-person cabins with sleeping space for two at 64 square feet each, and a larger shelter 100 square feet in size. Each cabin came with windows, a lockable door, power outlets, fold-up beds, built-in shelves, and heating and air-conditioning—all features included specifically from in-depth conversations with homeless populations. Each unit could be erected by a two-man crew in under an hour. The units were rented out for as low as $100 per month, with most residents remaining on-site an average of less than six months before moving on to larger, higher-grade, more permanent housing they could finally afford.

"That was our only site until 2019," says Amy. "Two years later, we were still trying to convince other cities this was a good idea. And they were like, 'I don't know.' And then COVID hit, and I'll be honest: it was a lucky strike. We were immediately relevant because cities had to physically distance people. The homeless populations couldn't be in congregate settings anymore. And that's why they initially bought our product. And then the model proved itself and we kept growing."

Today the for-profit Benefit Corporation has over 4,000 shelters built in the US and Canada with 121 sites across the US in 86 cities and 24 states.[5]

To achieve her goal of ending homelessness within her own lifetime, she knew she needed to accelerate the growth of her company by building her sphere of influence. The most effective way was to align interests with other stakeholders also interested in helping homeless populations. The business she started contributed one part to help solve her greater personal mission (the shelters), but she still needed the other puzzle pieces to come together to have a complete ecosystem. For example, the local city needs to donate land for the shelters. Not-for-profits are required to meet the counseling and mentorship needs of the newly housed population. Politicians help allocate resources, and they get to take the credit for "solving the homeless problem." As her influence grew, bringing together the stakeholders in each city became a key part of her growth strategy for Pallet.

Amy's main role, as the CEO, became political outreach to communities and cities, getting the word out about the sustainable model they've created that is helping uplift so many ex-cons and homeless people around the nation. "We want the world to see that peoples' futures are defined by their potential, not their past history," says Amy. "People are our bottom line. We invest in people and strive to build them up by providing meaningful, living-wage employment in a purpose-driven environment, building transitional shelters for displaced people who are in crisis."

When I asked Amy if she gets any pushback from people about creating a profitable business in the process, she just laughed. "I have a business and resources and investors behind me and the opportunity to leverage all of these things to drive toward creating even more solutions. Why wouldn't I do that if I can? There are so many social models that just don't work. What matters is getting all the resources pointed in the right direction and a framework laid out that we can actually implement to get to the end goal of benefitting people."

In Amy's situation, her many stakeholders benefit from joining together, but those stakeholders need to be organized and aligned. To insert her positive influence, Amy's role is to nurture this community, building her sphere of influence—and not just so she can sell more units. It helps her personal mission of ending homelessness in her lifetime. Each time she brings together groups of stakeholders that can mutually win from her solution, it makes the next project an easier sell. After doing it enough times, it almost becomes a plug-and-play process for success.

When building your sphere of influence, you need to be thinking about how you can multiply your efforts and who you can align with to execute your plan so that everybody wins. As Amy shared, "We didn't know that's what we would end up doing. We thought we would just produce a shelter and sell it. And that was it. And I can tell you right now, that's not all we do. Because if we did that, it would be unsuccessful. When you think about expansive thinking and social enterprise in general, which is what I'm passionate about, it's important to know who your stakeholders are. That's something I did not know when we started Pallet. I'm not a political person. I don't care about politics at all. I know nothing about it. And I spend most of my time today and in the last year hanging out with politicians and trying to convince them that this is a good idea.

"I find it kind of funny and ironic that you'll probably find yourself engaging with stakeholder groups that you never imagined you would. But the sooner you can acknowledge and identify and get to know those stakeholder groups, the better off you'll be in both learning about the market space but also penetrating the market space. You're really not going to get anywhere if you don't know who holds the power in those spaces."

Pallet's paying customers are typically cities, counties, states, and federal agencies. The actual users are people who have been displaced by homelessness or natural disasters. A third stakeholder group is the nonprofit service providers who run their sites and provide the services to the end user who utilizes their product.

"Our stakeholder group is really large and complex," says Amy. "We have to advocate for the success of our customers—the cities and townships. We have to advocate for the success of our service provider partners. And we have to advocate for the success of the end user. Often, those three groups are inherently in conflict with one another. So we're sort of this middle entity that goes, 'Look, we're providing a product here. But we also want to be sort of the glue that's bringing you all together in a productive way.'"

Exercise: Influencing Your Outer World

How will you build a valuable sphere of influence that contributes to your greater mission?

_____

_____

Connected to Your Customers

Don't forget about the people who use your products or services—they're a key part of your network too. Many folks in business overlook the importance of these relationships, thinking customers are just there to bring in money. But that's not the whole picture. It's crucial to put your customers' needs first and genuinely care about making their lives better. Just because you can sell something doesn't mean you should. When you keep your customers' best interests in mind, your decisions become clearer and more meaningful.

Finding the right way to help your customers can take time. For example, a Texas start-up was focused on building short courses to help lower-income workers gain more skills, mostly targeting the Spanish-speaking population. Although this low-income population was the end customer, they were not the paying customer. Instead, larger corporations purchased these courses and offered them as a benefit for their hourly wage workers, to skill up their workforce and keep jobs filled. The courses were well designed as short videos followed by a quiz so that the end customer fit in the learning during their work breaks, and the start-up worked with corporations to help define the coursework, as they paid for the service for their employees.

After several years in business, the management team at the start-up uncovered their real mission: helping lower-wage workers gain more financial stability. Their end customers needed to increase their income, which is why they engaged in the coursework the company offered through their employer. However, the employer wasn't necessarily focused on increasing their own workers' income; they wanted to retain their talent. Once the start-up decided to also embrace their end customers' deeper needs, all the coursework offered a pathway for greater earning potential, not just reskilling for a job with the same pay. Through this shift in their mission, the types of courses they offered changed. They were able to build a win–win–win model, with alignment among the start-up to earn revenue based on its mission, the corporations to retain talent, and the workers to increase income. Notably, delivering on their promise to their end customer enhanced their company reputation, making word-of-mouth marketing a mainstay of their business model.

Your Worthy Reputation

Building a solid reputation takes time, but it can unravel in an instant. Your network's strength relies heavily on your reputation, which is shaped by your actions. Working for companies that match your values boosts your credibility. On the flip side, aligning with unethical companies can harm it. Take Boeing, for example: recent safety issues exposed by whistleblowers have affected all Boeing employees' reputations.

A strong reputation opens doors. People are more likely to support and connect with you when they trust you. This trust is crucial, especially when you're aiming to make a positive impact. It's not only about what you do, but also how you do it. People want to see that you're genuine, have integrity, are dependable, and are ethical. They want to see you living your values, understand your intentions, and believe in your skills. When you've built a positive reputation, opportunities for collaboration with like-minded partners become realistic. It helps you make connections, and these connections are key to creating significant positive change as a Disruptor for Good.

A positive reputation also makes it easier to get people on board with your ideas, helping you drive the change you want to see. It expands your network, making people more willing to support and connect with you. Your reputation can even impact how people view the causes and organizations you're associated with, reflecting well on the issues you care about.

Additionally, if you have a track record of ethical behavior and positive contributions, people are more likely to forgive your mistakes. Being accountable, transparent, and owning up to your part goes a long way.

Your reputation is your most valuable asset in creating positive change.

Cultivate Positive Influences

Jim Rohn, businessman and personal development expert, says, "You are the average of the five people you spend the most time with."[6] And if you think about it, it makes sense. If your friends are setting ambitious goals for themselves, if they're contributing to the community, if they're interested in becoming a better human, that is what will rub off on you. And the opposite is true as well. If the people you spend the most time with feel unmotivated in life or are stuck in negative talk, you will pick this up too. Their values will subconsciously attach to you and become yours.

Exercise: Influencing Your Inner World

Who are the five people you spend the most time with?

_____

Are you happy being the average of those five people?

_____

What changes would you like to make?

_____

After reflecting on your current circle, consider who fits in with your desired contribution to the world. Who will help you—and even join you—on your journey up the Upward Spiral for Good? Do you share a common set of values? Are these people challenging themselves and you? Are you all continually growing? Embracing change? Those are the people who will energize you to keep moving forward toward your potential.

Collaborate and Connect, Instead of Compete and Repel

Alongside building your reputation and sphere of influence, fostering collaborative relationships will become an integral part of your daily efforts to create positive change across all aspects of business. Your success does not prevent the success of your peers, siblings, or community. It's just the opposite: your success can inspire others around you and vice versa.

When driven by a personal mission, your energy is channeled toward realizing the broader change you envision, motivating you to continually explore avenues that make a lasting difference. This collaborative mindset is not common in our current capitalistic system, but when your personal mission is bigger and more exciting than a single business, your drive to cooperate with other partners goes well beyond a balance sheet.

Allbirds, an eco-friendly shoe company started by New Zealander Tim Brown, demonstrates how a collaborate approach can help an entire industry. They created a tool that measures how much carbon their products use, spots problem areas, and helps cut down pollution. Instead of keeping this tool secret, Allbirds shared it with other fashion companies around the world. By doing this, their positive impact grows exponentially, and they become leaders in showing other companies what's important in the industry.

The company's press release clearly states the intention behind the action: "We know that sharing proprietary information might not make the most business sense. But the global climate crisis is bigger than business. And if competition got us into this mess, perhaps collaboration can get us out."[7]

The principle of a win-win collaborative solution strengthens relationships and most likely enhances the success of your personal mission. Working together often depends on uncovering common ground and aligning where possible so that all parties potentially grow through exchange. There is an African proverb that I was told growing up: if you want to go fast, go alone; if you want to go far, go together. That is what collaboration is about.

A Kinder Way

Kind Laundry is one of the fastest-growing ecological laundry detergent companies in Canada. They market eco-friendly, healthy, chemical-free detergent sheets that bypass the use of ecologically damaging plastic containers.

Coming from an immigrant family from Hong Kong, with English as his second language, Kind Laundry cofounder Bernard Law had to overcome many hurdles, including a lack of a safety net in his childhood to arrive at his current position as a successful eco-entrepreneur. Bullied and teased at school, he says he hated the whole educational process and that the experience gave him a basic distrust and dislike for people that took years to shake. His father was working around the clock, and his mother spoke hardly any English, so he was navigating his new environment alone. He felt very isolated and misunderstood at this time.[8]

In need of money, at the age of 16, he got his first part-time job planting trees for a not-for-profit organization in Canada. Since he'd immigrated, it was the first time that he was surrounded by overtly nice people who showed a genuine interest in him. They noticed he held back socially, and wanting more of him, they encouraged him to "come out of his shell." Bernard explained that being out in nature surrounded by kind people allowed him to finally let down his guard and relax for the first time since he left Hong Kong. Feeling appreciated and seen in that seemingly insignificant first job experience left a positive impression on him (and planted a seed of kindness and inclusion that would flourish in his coming years).

When he graduated from college with a degree in advertising, the supervisor at his first ad agency internship told him, "Hey, you're not cut out for this job. I think you really should go look for another career." He considered this feedback, but instead of quitting, he began thinking one step ahead about how to stand out and excel. It wasn't long before Bernard began to climb the corporate ladder in advertising, tapping into the resilience he had earned from his childhood. Soon, he was in a supervisory position, but unlike his past supervisor who had treated him poorly, Bernard made sure he encouraged others around him and built a strong teamwork ethic.

His team-building ability led to even more promotions, but it wasn't sufficiently satisfying. "I'd go after a raise and they'd give me a new title and a bigger office and all that—which is such a rip-off deal because my responsibility went up by 100% each time, but my salary would only go up by 10%, you know? After a couple of years, I was like, 'You know what? I can do so much more for myself. I'm outta here!'"

Wanting to build his own company, he took a risk by starting a franchise restaurant with his wife, Angie, but by the year 2020, they were both exhausted and heavily in debt. On top of everything else, both were shocked at the amount of single-use plastic containers and waste they were producing at the restaurant every day. Doing their personal and restaurant laundry, they were equally horrified at how bulky the laundry detergent bottles were and how much space they took up in recycling bins— contributing to the 630 million plastic detergent jugs that end up in US landfills every year.

"There are currently not many laundry options out there that are completely plastic-free and safe and healthy to use," explains Bernard. "If you picture the laundry aisle in any grocery store, it still looks like the same old laundry detergent aisle since we were all kids, right? When Angie and I discovered a new format—detergent sheets made from a mostly plant-derived formula—we just loved the whole eco-friendly concept of it. Being into sustainability, it aligned with who we are as people."

They sold the restaurant and put every dollar they had into starting Kind Laundry. Unlike most businesses, Bernard says, Kind Laundry has been totally self-funded and profitable since day one as they intelligently leveraged their deep expertise in online marketing. Now, they could take their hard-earned business skills, and Bernard's strength of resilience, and use them for good.

When I asked him what was one of the most important things he'd learned making the transition from the corporate world to a more global, kind venture, he didn't even hesitate. "No one individual can do all the work," he says. "It requires a village, a team to execute and lean on each other and trust each other. So that is the company culture that we have instilled into Kind Laundry." Because of his lived experiences, the value of their village was even more precious.

"We need the family environment because we're all in this together. We see each other at work more than we see our own family members. We actually have this culture where we've become very vulnerable with each other." Every other week, Bernard and Angie have a self-development day with their team in which they share personal and human stories and their motivations for what they want from life.

"If you're always only going for the dollar, at some point, that kind of burns out and there's just no purpose behind it. My main thing—especially with Kind Laundry—is always what is the 'why' of what you're doing. In the case of my business, what we're doing is always based on advancing the environment and people's health. Hearing, 'We just eliminated a quarter of a million plastic jugs in the landfill' is more exciting to me than hearing, 'We just made $250,000.' Money, to me, comes and goes. It flows. But the impact that you make on this world? That, to me, is more exciting." Through building his company Kind Laundry with his wife, Angie, Bernard created the safety net he missed out on during his childhood, which gives the company a distinct cultural advantage. And the strong community in turn drives their ongoing success.

Your Team for Success

On our path to achieving our personal mission, life happens. Launching a business is hard. Working on a team is hard. Working toward your personal mission is hard. None of us are exempt from hard times. In addition, all humans experience loss, disappointment, fear, sadness, and self-doubt. As you embark on your valuable work in the world, your life outside work happens in tandem. And the highs and lows that are the normal cycle of human existence impact how you can show up and relate to your work. Your inner circle and trampoline are essential. Prioritizing and nurturing your relationships is invaluable for an ambitious and worthwhile career.

But no one can change the world on their own, and as I'm sure you know by now, connections are a two-way street. All the relationships you embrace require a delicate balance of giving and receiving, like waves on the shore, rolling in and out continually. Not only will your connections bring you more opportunities, but they will also share different perspectives, they will help you grow what's possible as you combine your ambitions, and they will keep you moving forward when you need that extra push. From your safety net and trampoline, you receive support and also *energy*. You should be willing to return that energy with interest when you play it forward to your colleagues, employees, and mentees later on in your career. As your network becomes more robust over the years, something as simple as an introduction or a conversation can change a whole industry. Be open to letting your connections fuel your personal mission and vice versa. In order to create lasting, mutually beneficial connections with your network, you'll need to focus on positivity, on win-win outcomes, and on the greater good.

YOUR NEXT BIG MOVER

As you reflect on the insights and exercises from this chapter, consider the following: What is one powerful leap you can take to align your connections more fully with your desired contribution? What Big Mover action could propel you closer to utilizing your network in service of creating a positive impact?

Take a moment to capture your Big Mover in your workbook or the following.

_____

_____

_____

_____

_____

CHAPTER 7

YOUR CONFLICT

How will you clear your path when necessary?

WITHOUT A DOUBT, OUR WORLD needs more kindhearted people in positions of leadership, whether it be executives in C-suites, board rooms, government, or entrepreneurial leaders. And although it may seem obvious, these leadership roles require getting comfortable with being uncomfortable, plus learning how to navigate and lean into necessary challenges. Having worked with many people like Grace, I have noticed that embracing conflict can be counter to the very qualities that make her so valuable. However, working toward being a Well-Rewarded Disruptor, she needs to be able to advocate for what she wants and therefore to get proficient and comfortable with complex conversations that may be uncomfortable or may involve conflict. The question

I explore with clients is whether they are equipped to have the difficult conversations needed to achieve success and meet their potential as a future disruptor. Most of the time, the answer is some form of "not really," requiring some tools or a mindset shift to be set up for success.

The positive influencers among us are usually empathetic, generous, and thoughtful, although they are not immune to obstacles, stumbling blocks, and difficult interpersonal challenges. This is especially true if they have a personal mission that is driving them forward to achieve something powerful with strong values to uphold along the way. In fact, getting on course to be the Well-Rewarded Disruptor will require you to let go of the standard do-gooder identity, of looking after others while minimizing our needs and mission. If you are on your way to the Upward Spiral, you will have to get comfortable picking your mission over fulfilling the mission of others, which will mean getting familiar with disappointing people you care about from time to time. Although the shift is awkward, it often means letting go of being liked and embracing being respected instead.

Today, schools have made significant progress in early education, helping students become comfortable recognizing emotions—sad, angry, happy, worried—which is a helpful start. In my experience, many of the do-gooders such as Grace are deeply empathetic, with a strong self-awareness and self-reflection practices; you may already have this as one of your strengths. However, all through our education, we are rarely, if ever taught how to have effective and positive conflict. Perhaps we are familiar with using "I" statements, and maybe with how to apologize, but being a disruptor means that you will be disrupting existing cycles, established patterns, processes, and stakeholders. You will need more tools to navigate this thorny terrain. Ironically, it's not just learning to deal with the external landscape; we also need to learn to get out of our very own way. Many times, we are actually our own greatest obstacle.

Growth and progression in your career seldom follow a straight, clear path. Yet with resilience and a commitment to constructive dialogue, many of these obstacles you encounter can become opportunities in disguise. By exploring strategies for addressing setbacks and engaging in positive confrontations, you can achieve understanding and better outcomes for your career, your contribution, and your own well-being. By advancing skills to reframe problems, pose thoughtful questions, and find mutual solutions, you can develop your adaptability and better empathize with others over time. Approaching tension or roadblocks through this lens has the power to transform the trajectory of your professional pursuits. The approaches outlined here can help open doors when your forward movement feels hindered, leading to new possibilities for you to advance your personal mission, while leveraging your unique talents and influence.

Positive Conflict with Others

In school, we are never formally taught how to resolve conflict with others, even though it's essential and teachable to a large degree. Many children are not learning these skills at home either. The majority of us end up being poor communicators, often avoiding conflict altogether. As a professional, working toward being a confident, assertive communicator will enhance your potential as a leader (and it's kinder too). When I was becoming certified in coaching, one of the topics we covered in depth was nonviolent communication (NVC), an approach to interpersonal communication and conflict resolution created in the 1960s by clinical psychologist Marshall Rosenberg.[1] I found it enormously helpful because the structure makes difficult conversations seem approachable and less daunting. NVC involves both a philosophy and a set of skills to build understanding and find mutually acceptable outcomes focused on empathy and understanding.

Prior to understanding the NVC format, I had only experienced conflict as rigid, emotional, and met with defensiveness. Someone was right, and the other person was wrong, and it was difficult to emerge stronger together from this style of conflict. In contrast, using the NVC method has some clear benefits, including being able to reach your own personal mission without a wake of casualties along the way. Key principles include focusing on universal human needs, taking responsibility for one's reactions, and seeking a shared sense of purpose. You will inevitably disagree with someone on your team, a business partner, or perhaps even a lobby group trying to undo your important and valuable work. Becoming a Disruptor for Good means you will be disrupting the status quo—which will definitely ruffle some feathers, and you need to be prepared. Everyday issues are the starting place to practice the skills. Learning how to address these types of conflicts can help get you and your conflict partner on the same page much faster, often without hardship. Practice is mandatory, and the only way to skill up. From there, you can be proactive and use the same tools to deal with major obstacles in the way of your personal mission.

With the NVC method, there are four steps to tackle a difficult conversation:

OBSERVATION

Begin by observing the situation and describing it without judgment. It's as if you were describing a scene from a photo or video (something you can physically describe). It's harder than you think to do this and takes some getting used to. You will be surprised how often you are tempted to use subjective words. For example, if a coworker says to you, "I notice that you have been disengaged lately," that involves a judgment. What does *disengaged* even mean? And the meaning may be different for both people. Instead, they might say, "I noticed that you have not participated in the conversation in our morning meetings this week." This is an observation that you could actually watch in a movie, and it makes no assumptions about your reasons for the behavior or judgment about it. It allows for a better launching-off point for the conversation.

FEELING

Next, you express your feelings, focusing on your emotions, not the other party's, expressing your perspective through "I" statements: "I feel sad, angry, frustrated, irritated." Note that you don't want to use words that involve the other person, such as "I feel abandoned, I feel manipulated, I feel taken advantage of." If you find yourself using these words, look for what is underneath them. Instead of abandoned, maybe you feel anxious. Stick with the very source of the feeling that you are experiencing. (If you need help naming feelings, search images of a "feeling wheel" online, and many charts will appear for you to use as a resource.)

NEED

Then you clearly state your desired need from the other person. Articulate what you are hoping for from the other person: "Given the deadline, I need more hours of support for the project I am working on," or "I need to block off three days on my calendar without interruptions to finish the project." The more you know about your specific needs, the better you can communicate them. The transparency is helpful for everyone.

REQUEST

Finally, you deliver your request so that your *need* can be met. It should be very specific and actionable. It isn't a demand; the other person has a choice to say yes or no to your request. For example, "Would you consider letting me work from home this week to finish the presentation without normal interruptions from our teammates?"

Here's a different example from start to finish of the NVC process:

> "I have noticed that our meeting to review my work progress has been delayed twice (*observation*). I feel frustrated because, as more urgent things surface, it gets deprioritized (*feeling*), and I really want to touch base on my performance and possible promotion before the end of the year (*need*). Would you be willing to meet early one morning next week to make sure we get to it (*request*)?"

As you read through this, it may feel obvious or seem rehearsed. It is. You should rehearse each of the four steps until it becomes second nature. From what I have seen and experienced, as you master each of these steps, you gain a significant advantage in meeting your own objectives for your personal mission. These steps are harder than they first seem, and the majority of people you encounter will not know how to work in this framework. But just knowing your side of the equation is already helpful and will likely generate a better response from the other party.

If you encounter someone else conversing in this format, you can rely on this structure to listen for their observation, feelings, needs, and request. You can also probe further when it's not clear and ask questions such as "I hear that you want me to work harder. So that I understand what you want, what exactly does that look like to you?" Or you can repeat back to them what you have heard to make sure you understand them properly: "You want me to come earlier to work this week? What time are you hoping for?" When you repeat this back, the other person feels seen and heard. If you get it wrong, it's a perfect opportunity for them to reclarify, which is just as helpful. Learning this method will help prepare you for the obstacles you may encounter in fulfilling your personal mission.

KNOWING YOUR YES

Getting to Yes is the title of a bestselling book originally released in 1981 and since updated in two editions.[2] The key concept is very relevant to reaching your desired contribution and having a clear picture of what you want. Just as you need to be willing to have the hard conversations, it's equally important to know what to set aside, and let go. It is also important to avoid distractions; even if they may be worthy, they can pull you from your mission. *Getting to Yes* is about being intentional with your choices and staying focused on the prize—your *yes* (in our case, your personal mission). Once you know what you want to achieve in your career, you need to allocate your time to opportunities that move you forward. Your *yes* pulls you in the right direction. Life will present you with all sorts of distractions that seem equally important—but ultimately you have to allocate your time and preserve your focus. The more issues you take on, the more diluted your time becomes. Having a clear focus and personal mission makes it easier to narrow down to what is most valuable for you.

> # The more issues you take on, the more diluted your time becomes.

Jane Goodall has managed to stay focused on the well-being of animals throughout her career. She started by studying chimpanzees, but now she advocates for all animals on our planet. Her personal mission has kept her focused, and she has been able to deliver a significant contribution to our understanding of animal behavior in her lifetime. I'm sure she cares about many other things too, such as access to education, equal rights for women, and so on. However, although she may be helpful in those regards, she has closely chosen to prioritize her time advocating for the conservation of our planet and animal kingdom.

The *Getting to Yes* strategy is to know where you want to get to and to make sure your choices and battles are helping you get there. Saying no means being okay with disappointing others in service of your greater mission.

BE OPEN TO LETTING GO

When you are driving toward your personal mission, you deliberately pick a strategy to get there. Revisiting your strategy along the way is always valuable to make sure it is still your best approach. Sometimes, we confuse the strategy we selected with the mission itself. The clearest example is in US politics: as a citizen in the US, voting as a Democrat or a Republican is your strategy to achieve your desired outcome. What gets tricky is when your strategy becomes your identity. By limiting yourself to forever a Democrat or Republican, you make it very difficult to switch lanes if and when your values no longer align with that party or when there is a better way to achieve your ultimate vision. The same goes for the strategy you select to reach your personal mission. Be open to continually assessing the best strategy for your desired progress.

Optimal strategies for materializing your personal mission can and will shift, given new landscapes, relationships, and knowledge. Attach too tightly to one playbook, title, or organization, and you risk compromising the end goal in service of misplaced means. The flexibility to pivot in order to best align with your personal mission is key. Remember that no role or institution inherently constitutes your identity. Regularly connecting your choices back to your core motivations gives you freedom to evolve how you operate while remaining centered on your personal calling. As strategies stall or opportunities emerge, remain nimble to best serve the vision you have set. The core idea is that while your purpose should be steady, the processes for actualizing it demands responsiveness to growth and circumstances.

A lot of people spend 5, 10, 15, or more years in a profession or in a certain position, and even if they discover they really want to do something different, they figure it's too late to change course because they've gotten so far down that first road. This is what's known as the *sunk cost fallacy*. The thinking is that you've sunk so much time, effort, money, and identity going in one particular direction that it's not worth it to make a change. But nothing could be further from the truth, especially when your life circumstances change, opening up more freedom for you to follow your calling.

If you find yourself in this dilemma, do what Elspeth Jones, deputy CEO and strategic litigator at ClientEarth in the UK, did: "At the point of leaving university, my priority was financial stability," says Elspeth. "My parents separated when I was a teenager, and my father was really unwell. I had two younger sisters, and I was worried about their financial security and my mum's, as well as my own. Having done a law degree and a master's in law at Oxford, I made a beeline for the commercial law world, because that's where the money was."

Elspeth spent five years studying law, passed her bar exams, and then another six years practicing as a commercial barrister in London. She built out her client base, creating a niche for herself while taking on increasingly bigger, more lucrative cases. "I was working so hard that I didn't have the headspace to look up at the rest of the world," she says. "But as I approached my thirties, I started coming up for air, looking around and reconnecting with some earlier passions, especially the natural world. I learned how to scuba dive and just fell in love with the underwater world. Then I started picking up books about the environment and climate change, and I reached a point where I could clearly see the climate and biodiversity crises looming. Once I could see it, I couldn't unsee it. Up to that point I'd naively assumed that somebody out there in the world was dealing with those things, that somebody had it all figured out and under control already. But it became really clear to me that they didn't.

"I was making good money but had accidentally built a niche in oil rig and oil tanker litigation. I had blueprints of oil rigs all over my office walls, and I suddenly saw this juxtaposition between my day-to-day work and where my heart really was. It just clicked. And I was like, 'Ah ha! Okay. This is why I'm not feeling fulfilled. There's a complete mismatch between how I spend my 90,000 hours and what I really care about in the world.' And that was when I made the move into the space that I'm in now."

In 2014, Elspeth left commercial law and took an unpaid internship at the London offices of ClientEarth, an environmental law charity holding governments and corporations accountable for climate change, nature loss, and pollution. "The organization was only five years old then, so it was still young and growing rapidly. By this stage of my career, I had a financial safety net, my sisters were in jobs, and everything was much more secure. So I made the leap. I could see people who were maybe three to five years ahead of me in their legal careers, and they had reached a point where they had bought a big house and were hugely committed to a mortgage. They had children in expensive schools, and they couldn't change paths if they wanted to, because they needed the salary. I realized if I was going to leave, it had to be then—before I locked myself into a lifestyle that I wouldn't be able to afford on another salary."

And ten years later, Elspeth has made her way from intern to deputy CEO at ClientEarth, with the organization growing from 45 people to nearly 300 people in that time. Is she happy that she made the change? "Absolutely!" she says. "I have never looked back. Every day I feel that strong sense of purpose—that I am making an impact on the world, that I'm working on something really important and making a contribution that is much bigger than myself. I suppose there is something in there about legacy—wanting to do more good than harm in my lifetime and to try to play a part in nudging society onto a more sustainable path. It has also been an incredible adventure. Taking this path has opened up so many new things for me, which I'm immensely grateful for."

GETTING IT RIGHT

When we confront obstacles and disagreements, our instinct is often to focus intently on proving ourselves correct to eliminate any wrongness. However, this *being right* mindset can come at the expense of truly understanding others, and at times even distorts the truth through our self-interested lens. An alternative approach is to shift into *getting it right* mode with a genuine commitment to discovery: asking curious questions, creating space for shared meaning, and attending precision instead of defending entrenched positions. Leadership expert Peter Drucker said, "Management is doing things right; leadership is doing the right things."[3] He wisely suggested that *getting it right* is more valuable than *being right*. To navigate the difference of these two phrases, it helps to be in service of a bigger mission that requires your best-nuanced judgment.

As we tackle thorny topics with colleagues, the goal isn't always to resolve differences through a binary right-or-wrong verdict. Often staying open-minded to improve collective understanding helps move the needle more meaningfully. By letting go of our angle as the only angle, we create potential for innovative solutions. Being receptive and discerning may not satisfy our ego like dominating debate, but it empowers owning and advancing truth together.

The key distinction here is that being right serves the self, while getting it right serves the shared purpose and broader truth. This matters deeply in how we approach conflict.

FAILURE IS YOUR FRIEND

Failure is not often talked about as an asset. As well, most people are afraid to make themselves vulnerable by sharing their failures. And yet failures are actually your fastest portals to success and getting it right. As Paolo Coelho, Brazilian best-selling author, puts it, "The secret of life is to fall seven times and to get up eight times."[4]

This concept of failing forward—emphasizing the positive aspect of failure and the potential for self-reflection, growth, and progress—can result in moving forward with renewed knowledge and resilience. Another way of looking at this is practicing iterations—the cycle of try–fail–evaluate–redesign–try–fail–evaluate–redesign, rinse and repeat. In other words, "If at first you don't succeed, try, try again."

Yes, failure is frustrating. But each time you go back and incorporate the feedback, you end up with a better version of both you and your creation. And each time you get feedback, it feels less and less personal. Your ego gets out of the way, and you can make huge strides forward, thinking big more effectively.

Conflict with Yourself

Organizational psychologist and author Adam Grant says, "Hiding your weaknesses doesn't project strength. It reflects insecurity. No matter what you do, people who know you well will find your flaws. You might as well get credit for having the humility to look for them, the self-awareness to see them, and the integrity to admit them."[5]

For many of us, our biggest opportunities are accessible if we get out of our own way. The good news is you only have to convince one person—you—to do this. As we mature and move through our careers, the same tools that we utilized to survive in our youth can limit our success and desired fulfillment. Do-gooders specifically are susceptible to covering all the bases and going above and beyond in a team dynamic, working on overdrive, and picking up the pieces of any underperforming teammate or partner. In my first full-time job out of college, in consumer technology in Silicon Valley, I prided myself on the fact that they needed to hire three people to replace me when I left three years later. I was raising my hand for everything on our team, and although I was looking like a great teammate on the surface, I was preventing the others on my team from developing the necessary skills. Eventually, I was exhausted. I was chief of picking up the extra pieces so that I could be the most useful employee instead of focusing on my desired personal mission—or, at least, the business mission. What starts off as a one-time fill-in can quickly become a role that you take on, which, of course, is not usually compensated. I see this pattern of overachievement in many do-gooders too, especially women. And it does not usually get you where you want to be.

With my coaching clients, I have found the fastest and easiest way to identify how you become your own saboteur is by taking the Positive Intelligence test.[6] It takes about 15 minutes of your time. Just like any other test, the results are not facts about you but an interpretation that may be helpful. These saboteurs are something we can directly influence. Shirzad Chamine, the author of *Positive Intelligence*, points out that internal saboteurs often start off as our guardians to help us survive the real and imagined threats to our physical and emotional survival as children. "By the time we are adults, we no longer need them," he writes, "but they have become invisible inhabitants of our mind."[7] Turning down the volume on your saboteurs is not an overnight process. But if you practice, you can become more skilled and learn to identify them easily as they show up. And you can see them in others too.

Our saboteurs serve us until they don't, and that's when we need to grow beyond them. A perfect example is my 25-year-old client Eric. He took the Positive Intelligence saboteur quiz, and like most of my clients, he felt the results were thought provoking and seemed accurate. But his feelings about them were mixed. When life gets challenging, Eric buckles down into hyperachieving mode while overfocusing on getting everything right. He likes and relies on this saboteur, because it propels him to rise to the top of his game and achieve. Despite English being his second language, this combo got him a scholarship to a US university and helped him graduate at the top of his class in his graduate school program. However, as he's getting older and looking deeper, he is aware of how these saboteurs drive him to continually ignore the physical signs of stress on his body as he continues to relentlessly push through. He often feels exhausted and misses the playful and lighthearted part of himself, which he deprioritizes for his version of success. Not surprisingly, his body is paying attention even if his head is not: he was recently diagnosed with chronic fatigue and irritable bowel syndrome.

After becoming aware of his saboteurs, instead of struggling with burnout and health issues, he's finally managing them by prioritizing what is most important to him for reaching his personal mission and limiting what he says "yes" to. He has also prioritized healthy ways to recharge. And although it has not been easy, he consciously seeks less outside validation. His mantra is to work smarter, not harder.

Our brains have a natural plasticity that can facilitate literally changing our minds. We may have had self-limiting thoughts for years, but the brain's ability to rewire its neural connections into new patterns makes it possible to change old mental patterns in as little as 40 days. All it takes is awareness and the sincere desire to shift.

Catch those saboteur thoughts, and then use some of the following tools Chamine uses to overcome saboteurs:

- Empathize: Give yourself some grace and compassion.
- Explore the situation: Be curious.

- Innovate: Come up with creative new solutions.
- Navigate: Find your path in a new direction.

Once you know your saboteurs, you can recognize them in others as well. But when you see them, try not to be critical. Instead, recognize that the person is not feeling safe and is therefore not in a position to rise above self-sabotage. Respond in a way that puts them at ease instead of attacking or judging them and driving them into an armored position. Being someone who can tap into people's potential and evoke their better selves is a hugely important skill that will set you up for much success. You can literally change group dynamics by switching people out of a negative nosedive into a positive Upward Spiral.

Exercise: Reflections

In the workbook record your top saboteurs, and keep an eye out for them.

_____

_____

_____

YOUR IMPOSTER SYNDROME
MAY BE PIONEER SYNDROME

One thing that often comes up when coaching clients is what's called *imposter syndrome*. So many people have great ideas for totally new business models and about how their products or services will change lives. But then they sell themselves short, saying something like, "Who am I to start this business?" or "What am I thinking? I don't have the experience to pull this off!" To subconsciously put the brakes on, we get in our own way by procrastinating. Perhaps we feel like we may not perform well enough, aiming for perfection to delay getting going and stalling, finding a reason to stop our progress. All these issues can be worked on by being conscious of these behaviors and potentially having a sense of humor when you become aware of them. In addition to awareness, setting small milestones to keep you moving forward can be helpful too.

However, my own coach shared her wisdom with me that often, what is originally thought of as imposter syndrome when doing good in the world is more like pioneer syndrome.[8] I believe humans' most interesting advantage is the ability to continually explore and imagine. We are always pushing the limits and imagining something that has never been done before. Creating original work and putting it out into the world requires vulnerability, and it can be challenging. If you're determined to contribute and do things differently, you're always going to feel a little uncertain and a bit unqualified as you charter new territory. It's normal and part of the job requirement. If this is you, don't let your fears stand in the way, since what you have to offer the world is unique and valuable. Feeling uncomfortable is just the standard cost of entry for doing something new and impactful.

HANDLING SETBACKS AND BUILDING RESILIENCE

Life's biggest challenges are also life's greatest growth opportunities. Getting told no and having doors closed for something you strongly believe in can be disheartening. But being crystal clear on your contribution gives you tremendous motivation and determination to align on what you want to achieve and draw strength from it to try again.

There is a window of opportunity to get valuable insights when the doors are not opening. For example, if you are pitching a client, and they have just told you that you are not going to get the contract, it's time to ask questions and be curious. "What is one thing you would have liked to have seen that would have strengthened my pitch?" "What is your greatest concern in working together?" "What would have helped you say yes?" When you hear their answer, repeat it back to make sure you really got it. And then follow up to keep the door open. If they gave you feedback, show them you have taken it to heart. Often, staying in the conversation actually allows the next opportunity to work out. Working with someone open, curious, and coachable is very attractive, and therefore, how you handle the first setback is actually an opportunity to show your character.

Asking for Help

Solving important problems means you will need to have a handful of guardian angels who look after you. As we discovered in our conversation about connections, your network and the community of people around you are critical in realizing your ambitions. There is no doubt that asking for help from your community—and even strangers—will need to become a mainstay in your strategy. People love helping others, especially when they are specific about what they need, and they are willing to do the follow-up required to get the help implemented.

In conclusion, navigating conflict is an essential skill for anyone striving to make a positive impact. By embracing techniques like nonviolent communication, staying focused on your goals, being open to change, and learning from failure, you can transform challenges into opportunities for growth and progress. Remember that preventing conflicts from escalating is just as important as resolving them; setting clear expectations, maintaining open communication, and addressing issues promptly can go a long way in maintaining harmony. As you encounter successful examples of conflict resolution, take note of the strategies employed and consider how you can adapt them to your own situations. Most importantly, recognize that healthy conflict can be a catalyst for innovation, stronger relationships, and personal development. By viewing conflict as an opportunity to learn, grow, and find mutually beneficial solutions, you'll be better equipped to handle the challenges that arise on your path to making a meaningful difference in the world.

YOUR NEXT BIG MOVER

As you reflect on the insights and exercises from this chapter, consider the following: What is one powerful way you can lean into necessary conflict in service of your personal mission? What Big Mover action could propel you closer to utilizing these skills in service of creating positive impact?

Take a moment to capture your Big Mover in your workbook or on the following lines.

_____

_____

_____

_____

CHAPTER 8

YOUR CHALLENGE

How are you thinking big?

"I'M VERY CONTENT AND GRATEFUL about all the things I've seen and accomplished in life so far. But I can't help but wonder what my life would be like now if I'd set forward an even more ambitious vision for myself back then."

This is an actual quote from a colleague of mine. By all accounts, he has had a very successful and satisfying career. But this sentiment is common among ambitious professionals toward the end of their career journey, when they realize they were capable of *more* but they are now running out of time. They feel that they've left potential on the table. And it's not just to be busy and do more; instead, they realize that they had an even deeper, more profound potential within them.

Maybe this hindsight regret is inevitable to some degree for all of us. However, I'm a big believer in gathering wisdom from elders. You can take advantage of their insight now, while you are building momentum in your early years. Imagine how much further you can go in your impactful career if you embrace the challenge now—if you maximize your impact by going beyond the obvious.

Grace, for example, has already contributed to the positivity in the world through her first five years of work. But she has seldom taken the time to think about her career with a bird's eye view. In your wildest dreams, how do you want to spend your 90,000 hours, and how do you hope to change the world? Taking time to imagine our dreams—without constraints—helps you build a career that's worth you and your time.

In addition, in talking to the career superstars that I interviewed for this book, I have been impressed with their boldness and bravery in forging pathways that do great things for the world and for themselves. They think big and welcome challenges into their lives, overcoming obstacles. They are often audacious. When you know what you are working toward and why you are doing it, you can really tap into your greatness. It's contagious and often a catalyst for additional impact too.

This challenge is not about running faster on the hamster wheel, chasing endless achievement. I advocate for keeping life balanced, not for spinning the wheel of pointless aspiration. Our aim is to find a pathway that is *worth* your time (good for both you and the world). The challenge supports that aim by encouraging you to take on more only when it aligns with your ultimate goal—enhancing your contribution. The right challenge can create more flow, ease, and alignment, and it should ideally lead to more satisfaction. It may even bring an abundance of joy, fun, and harmony to your life. The idea is to work smarter versus working harder.

Bravery Zones

Yes, being brave and courageous is a generally desired and rewarding state to be in, but it does not always feel within reach. No one stays in that state throughout their lives. Life constantly throws us challenges, some are part of normal life development and growth, and other challenges are unique to our experience. During these waves, I have observed that there are three distinct bravery zones that we enter in and out of depending on where we are in life and what we need.

RESTORING

The first is the restoring or resting stage. It is where we go when life is particularly harsh. Choosing to rest often requires bravery and intentionality, as stopping our momentum feels counterproductive. However, while restoring or resting may feel like a retreat, it can be a space that heals, provides clarity, and strengthens us. This nurturing zone allows you to be thoughtful, prioritize, reassess your goals, and recover from any burnout.

There are times when entering a restoring phase is necessary due to illness, burnout, or mental health struggles. Recognizing the need to rest is a bold act that reflects our values and self-care priorities. It's crucial to visit this space when needed. The restoring zone is not a place where you have the emotional resources to give to others; instead, it is a place to replenish your emotional reserves. This equips you to return to a place where you can give. When your reserves are filled, you can move into the next zone to continue investing in your potential.

ACTIVE

In the next zone, you are emerging into your potential. We can boldly push ourselves in this active zone and handle more challenges. We are up for learning new skills and developing ourselves. Not only that, but we are also confident enough to step outside our safety zone and willing to try something new, even if it scares us. In this zone, we lean toward growth, saying yes to opportunities, and no to things that are not serving us. We embody a bold and opening stance to welcome valuable people, opportunities, and ideas. Many of us spend most of our time here. It feels good, steady, and reliable, but it is not necessarily magical.

EXPANDING

This third zone is rare: expansion. Few can sustain a state of expansion and confidence for long, but I believe we flow between all three zones in short and long cycles. In the expansion zone, you can elevate your personal mission like never before, being deliberate and bold in pursuing for your dreams. You embody ambition, with the wind at your back giving you an extra boost. You feel fearless in embracing the unknown and are often rewarded with a flow state in your work—feeling fulfilled and confident. People are drawn to your presence. This phase is intentional, marked by a belief in abundance and the power to achieve your goals.

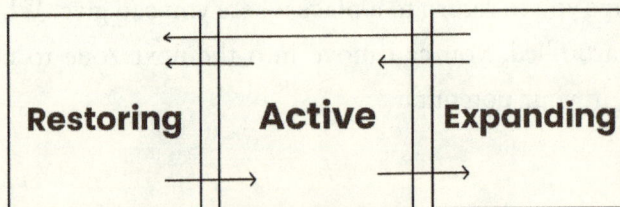

Figure 8.1. Bravery Zones

We're not always in a frame of mind to take on big challenges, especially with what's already on our plate. The restorative space is an invaluable place for recharging, although it takes courage to recognize its purpose and enter it for rest. This zone doesn't allow for new challenges, as we're often weary (although some people seem to pull off astounding miracles in the worst of times). In the active zone, you'll find comfort and contentment. However, if you notice yourself craving more excitement, it's time to test the expansion waters. In this expansion phase, you are best equipped to think bigger than ever, making brave and bold decisions—and it pays off.

Time, Energy, and Drive

Doing more good in your career usually does not mean harder work or more hours. It can boil down to your values, methods, and approach when it comes to business.

For instance, Sami Inkinen from Virta works hard and is boldly ambitious, often frequenting the expansion zone. But it does not cost him more personally than if he were in the active zone. He still has a spouse, kids, hobbies, trips, and weekends to enjoy many aspects of his life. The challenge of embracing the expansion zone is not meant to overwhelm your life with constant work; it's to maximize the efficiency of impact, to make your contribution larger without increasing your stress, time commitment, or energy levels.

If Sami Inkinen had set up a local diabetes clinic serving one community, he would likely be working just as many hours as a manager of the clinic, versus his role as CEO of a multibillion-dollar company reversing diabetes and obesity in millions of people already. He changed his work approach, not the amount of it so that he could create a larger contribution. He championed conflict

> The boldness of your vision is not correlated to the hours or energy required from you.

areas, embraced a network that aligned with his vision, and forged avenues for expansion.

The boldness of your vision is not correlated to the hours or energy required from you. But it does involve bravery, and that is not always easy to embody. Being aware of these three zones allows us to be more intentional about our mission.

From Very Small to Very Big

Khan Academy, a nonprofit headquartered in California, is a perfect example of someone taking an interesting idea and expanding it into an audacious, oversized (yet achievable) dream. Khan Academy's founder, Salman Khan, was able to greatly surpass his competitors and became the clear market leader due to the company's clever nonprofit structure.[1]

Sal was born and raised in New Orleans. His mother was born in Calcutta, India, and his father was born in Barisal, Bangladesh. His international family shaped his perspective on educational opportunities. A former hedge fund analyst with degrees from MIT and Harvard, Sal began remotely tutoring his cousin Nadia in August 2004. She was struggling in her math class, and it was holding her back from being placed in a more advanced math track. Since Nadia was in New Orleans and Sal was in Boston, he started tutoring her over the phone and on Yahoo Doodle after work.[2]

As Nadia improved, word got around and Sal started tutoring a handful of his other cousins and young family members. By 2006, scheduling had become a real issue, and he decided to record videos and post them on YouTube so everyone could watch at their own pace. This would vastly expand his potential impact—beyond what he could ever do in one-on-one tutoring sessions. Word spread, and more and more people started watching.

In 2008, the organization was incorporated as a 501c(3) nonprofit. It was not an easy decision. "I remember when Sal was starting," says Jeremy Schifeling, marketing director for Khan Academy. "He had this choice: Do I want to raise a bunch of venture capital, incorporate, and do all that stuff? That's what so many of his peers did. That's what Sebastian Thrun did with Udacity. That's what Daphne Koller did with Coursera. And now, we have probably 10 times the impact of any of those platforms because he made a decision (that he got criticized for at the time), which is he was going to give it all away for free.

"And just through the virtue of Google SEO, through YouTube, through all these platforms, we now can reach 150 million learners around the world with a staff of a small high school."

After starting the nonprofit, Sal continued to work on building Khan Academy during his spare time. Finally, in 2009, he quit his hedge fund job to pursue growing the academy full-time. He lived off his savings until he started to receive significant donations and grants from well-established philanthropic organizations, such as the Gates and Musk Foundations, grants that enabled him to hire more people and build out an ever-larger organization based around a few solid principles:

- Learner-centric content
- Accurate, world-class educational materials
- Diversity and inclusion

- Appropriate context
- Editorial integrity

"It all goes back to impact," says Jeremy. Sal's challenge to himself was to reach as many students as possible. He was successful, and that success translated to more funding and a reach that continued to expand. As of April 2024, the Khan Academy channel on YouTube has 8.36 million subscribers, and Khan Academy videos have been viewed well over two billion times. Lessons are available with subtitles and have also been translated into several languages, making them even more accessible.

In line with its values, Khan Academy also has a section dedicated to SAT preparation, the standardized test that is often used for college admissions in the United States. This levels the playing field, giving less advantaged students the opportunity to compete with students attending better schools and thus receiving a higher quality education.

For his part, Jeremy had a similar challenge: how to teach without being in a school. "When I was a substitute teacher," he says, "I sucked at teaching. I was yelling at kids. It was like all my worst moments happened in the classroom because I was trying to force the square peg (me) into a round hole (classroom teaching)." So he looked for a new way to teach. "All that time," he says, "I actually had these superpowers that were outside the classroom—things like scaling up ideas, building new organizations from scratch, right? But it took me a while to realize that if I actually wanted to do the most good in the world, I couldn't fit it into that narrow box of, 'I must be a teacher in this classroom for the next 40 years.' It took a while to find a way to play to my strengths based on the reality of the world and all the options out there."

By setting a truly audacious challenge for themselves, Sal, Jeremy, and the Khan Academy employees have reached billions of students. They could not have done this without seeing beyond perceived limitations. "I feel like people have this idea that you have to have a career that fits into a neat little box," Jeremy says. "Either you'll be an entrepreneur going to Silicon Valley, raising venture capital, or you have to be like an office drone, doing someone else's bidding every single moment of every single day. But we're all kind of these complex, weird individuals. We have different interests. We have different motivators and drivers.

"I like this idea of a portfolio career where I think people should consider, 'Hey, how do I have it all?' Plus, I think the reality is, there's so many curve balls in life, you just never know when things will change." Seeing—and embracing—the challenge before him let Jeremy reach beyond his expectations. "And now, here I am, at Khan Academy, doing something I'm really good at and love!"

When you decide to tackle a problem, sometimes imagining it even bigger than it is today can help discover the solution or possibility. In World War II, Dwight D. Eisenhower coordinated the largest military undertaking ever with the D-Day invasion of Normandy. He not only managed huge sea, air, and land forces, but also accounted for unpredictable weather, as well as the political wills of Roosevelt, Churchill, and de Gaulle.

Eisenhower said, "Whenever I run into a problem I can't solve, I always make it bigger. I can never solve it by trying to make it smaller, but if I make it big enough, I can begin to see the outlines of a solution."[3]

Eisenhower's approach to problem-solving is unique and made him a successful leader in many different settings. The "Eisenhower Principle" he outlines remains relevant and applies directly to business strategy management and leaders today.

Milestones and Flow

Just as it is important to normalize the setbacks that we looked at in the previous chapter on conflict, it's equally important to take the time to celebrate the wins along the way, both small and large. Recognize your progress, and let the joy, pride, and excitement linger. It is part of the reward system (or compensation) that gives energy back to you. Acknowledging your achievements in a way that feels authentic for you allows you to reflect on your learnings, and it fuels your motivation. Don't skip this part!

A hint that you are in the expansion zone and can produce your best work is when everything seems to flow. We all experience a flow state in our lives from time to time, some more than others. It could be as a child building a sandcastle on the beach or working in Indonesia with children at the Green School as a volunteer. It is a psychological state characterized by complete absorption in, focus on, and enjoyment of an activity. It's a mental state where you are fully immersed in what you are doing, often losing track of time and experiencing a deep sense of concentration and fulfillment. Even though you're working hard, you feel a sense of effortlessness and pride over what you've overcome. Your gifts are in sync with your efforts. You let go and are less self-conscious, creating a sense of freedom. Most importantly, you are deeply enjoying your work, can celebrate your achievements, the journey you are on, and the challenge before you.

By knowing when you are in the frame of mind to lean into challenging yourself and then knowing how to do it in a way that works for you, you are geared for greater presence and even more alignment. The good that you create for both you and the world becomes a catalyst for even more positivity, and it spirals upward to become exponential.

Leveling Up

Most people I have worked with underestimate their potential. We naturally calculate our potential based on where we are currently, instead of deciding from the top down where we want to be, regardless of circumstance. Starting from where you're at may help you reach, say, 10% further than you are now. However, embracing the challenge of worldwide change can increase that contribution tenfold.

To make it tangible, let's say your first job was not very inspiring, but you learned some office skills. It was nothing that you will cherish but was generally okay. Your goal for your next job should not be 10% better than "generally okay." Why settle for just a 10% better? Why not shoot for your ideal? It's relevant to how you spend your work hours—or your life hours, for that matter. Doing 10% better each time may be rewarding at the moment, but you could be shooting for 1,000%. You could ask yourself, *What have I got to lose?* But you could just as easily ask, *What have I got to gain?* If you are bold and brave and reach for an impossible dream and only ever reach 70% of what you envisioned, you're still far beyond 10% better than *okay*.

Don't worry about it feeling unrealistic or unlikely. If you can imagine it, you can make it happen. Knowing this, let's revisit your personal mission. Reread what you have so far. Now let's see if you can dream bigger. If you are feeling the expansion or even a seed of it, it will likely require you to expand your thinking on all the chapters you have already read. Finding the right level is a little like Goldilocks; you will need to discover the intensity that is just right for you so that you can maintain an overall balance of good for you and for the world and sustain your interest in that great work over a long period.

You do that through constant experimentation. For example, notice the subtleties of your contribution, of how you are uniquely gifted, and then lean into them one by one in your work. A favorite question that I have for interviewing someone is, "Beyond the job description, what else do you bring to the table that we should know and celebrate?" Keep asking yourself this question. Stay curious, and invest in your professional development. This will require a willingness to think differently, individually, and to break from the status quo.

Could you add one, two, or three zeros at the end of the number of people you are positively impacting, without compromising value? Or your own well-being? How would that change your work strategy? Is that something you are willing to try? Challenging yourself will ensure you are always contributing value to your cause and to the people around you. Instead of simply finishing a project on time or doing your job well, challenge yourself to make a positive impact and leave a lasting legacy through your work.

What would a leveled-up version of a sphere of influence look like for you? How could that be an advantage to the work you do? What would it look like to further benefit your customer base? How would it help you provide for their needs? Who in your life will embrace the challenge alongside you and say, "Of course" or "That makes total sense" if you share your personal mission with them? Challenge yourself to keep having conversations with people who have different perspectives or beliefs than you.

Being open to a greater challenge means letting go of your personal saboteurs. It means allowing yourself to have less control, but that also means you can have more ease, energy, and flow. Have you heard the saying "If you knew it would all work out, what would you do differently?" Accessing and believing in that premise allows us to reach for our potential. To benefit from this challenge when it arises, take the leap that it's all going to work out.

YOUR NEXT BIG MOVER

As you reflect on the insights and exercises from this chapter, consider the following: What one powerful step will launch you into a larger dream than you originally thought yourself capable of? What Big Mover action could propel you forward in service of creating positive impact?

Take a moment to capture your Big Mover in your workbook or on the following lines.

_____

_____

_____

_____

CHAPTER 9

YOUR COMMITMENT

How will you take action and build momentum?

A GO-GETTER CLIENT OF MINE in her mid-twenties energetically asked me before we started her coaching sessions what books she could read to get prepared and make the most of our work together. I didn't even get a chance to answer before she quickly mentioned a list of books she had read already to help her understand business leadership, philanthropy, and helpful work habits.

I followed up by asking her, "What are the most important things you've learned from those books so far? And what have you done with all that information?"

She thought about it for a second, then laughed and answered, "Well, it's all in the back of my head somewhere!"

She is not alone (and I am guilty too). We are in the age of extreme information consumption. We absorb new content all the time. Podcasts. Books. TikTok. Instagram. Netflix. Most of us are so busy taking in so much new content we never actually reflect on it, process it, or use it in our lives. For me, much of the content I consume does not stick with me beyond the moment of consumption. That's not because I am disinterested, but because I seem to have too many inputs, and it's easier to keep consuming than to actually work through and apply the valuable content to my life. We're becoming information junkies, getting our quick fixes, our next dopamine hit, just seeing the new stuff. And then it's on to the next tidbit and the next.

> Most of us are so busy taking in so much new content we never actually reflect on it, process it, or use it in our lives.

At the minimum, just knowing that your career will likely be 90,000 hours is an important mindset switch to start paying attention to how you are spending that time to make it *worth it*. But if you are inspired to explore your potential in a deeper way, you will be well served digesting the content, reflecting on how it applies to you, and taking steps to build your internal inertia. As author Sarah Ban Breathnach stated, "The world needs dreamers, the world needs doers, but above all dreamers who do."[1]

Be the dreamer who does. In this chapter, we pull together all your insights so that you can see all your reflections and ideas in one view. All the previous work you have completed sets you up for action, making it manageable, purposeful, and directed. After taking stock of all you have created so far, we will begin to design your plan of action—which includes a recap of all the work you have completed in each chapter. This includes your clear vision of where you want to go (your personal mission), the big steps you want to take to get you there (which I call your Big Movers), and finally the detail on how you will grow forward through experiments you will prioritize each quarter (Experiments in Action).

How to Get There

It takes both motivation and discipline to actually change your course for good. Throughout this book, you have been building the *motivation* you need to create a meaningful and ambitious career. Maybe you are excited to lean into your strengths. Or fired up to focus on what you really care about in the world. Or perhaps you are most excited to build your sphere of influence. Unfortunately, motivation alone is not usually sufficient to see the results you will be looking for over the long term—your whole career. You will also need to consistently show up for your personal mission too, which is where *discipline* comes in. Paring motivation with discipline is the best path to the most rewarding results. Remember, by analyzing your capabilities and your contribution, you are ready to answer *what* you want to do with your hours, and *why* it's important to you. Through discipline—planning and action— we determine *how* you are going to get there.

Before you can embark on any action steps, you must be really clear about where you want to be heading: What do you want to experience? What do you want to offer the world? Having clarity about this, which you've built up as you've worked through our exercises, makes it so much easier for the other pieces to fall into place. Just by doing that, you are already setting yourself far apart from most people and positioning yourself for a fulfilling career.

I have found that focusing on your desired growth is more relevant than a particular goal (although they could be interchangeable). That means prioritizing continuous learning, development, and progress rather than merely reaching target goals. Emphasizing growth means embracing the journey and finding fulfillment in the process of improving and evolving, both personally and professionally. In my case, if I focused on a goal, it would be to complete the writing of my first book by a certain date. In contrast, by focusing on growth, I aim to enjoy all the stages of learning and connecting with new people from the process too, to become an author. It's an ongoing commitment to be able to land my message with a willing and receptive audience. I am constantly seeking advice and resources to help me get better at the craft of writing. The journey itself is rewarding—not just reaching completion.

As you go through the following exercises to affirm your commitment to your growth, focus on being intentional with your pathway ahead. The more you can visualize yourself living in the Disruptor for Good quadrant, the more likely you will get there. Whenever you run into bumps in the road or have doubts—close your eyes and tap into the visualization of having already succeeded in your wishes. Feel that success in your body. Then mentally capture that sentiment like you would a photograph to refer back to when you need inspiration.

COMMITMENT TO BECOMING A DISRUPTOR FOR GOOD

The role models I interviewed for this book, both entrepreneurs and those who work within an organization, are all intentional with their careers, and their greater missions. Many of them set time aside to consciously design their plans for their lives and careers. I have a structure that will help you move closer to building a career that's impactful and rewarding.

Here's the catch: it will take some time to answer all the questions and get yourself set up for success, and then regular check-ins to make sure you are following your strategy effectively. But the payoff for being intentional with your time will be worth it, and exponential. To loosely paraphrase a quote attributed to Abraham Lincoln about spending the necessary time to sharpen an axe before attempting to chop down a tree, this reflective work, and the time it takes, sharpens your axe. The commitment process leverages the work you have already read in the previous chapters, bringing it all together. It will involve iterations, changes, and evolution—and that's all okay and expected.

To take the learning from this book and integrate it into your day-to-day routine, instead of just reading another book, it's time to fill in your answers to help you design your strategy for building inertia into your plan. Remember, you will miss 100% of the shots you don't take.

The following is a six-step commitment process that captures your intentionality for *Work That's Worth It*. Steps 1–3 draw upon your motivation, and steps 4–6 offer you a method that requires discipline. As you review and record your answers, remember Chapter 8, "Your Challenge"—make note of where you can push yourself healthily, so that your vision can be more expansive.

Step 1: Your Personal Mission

Capture your personal mission (see Chapter 4, "Your Contribution"). You will review this mission every two to five years, but it may well last a lifetime.

```
┌─────────────────────────────────────────────────────┐
│                                                     │
│                                                     │
│                                                     │
│                                                     │
└─────────────────────────────────────────────────────┘
```

Remember, it may be only one or two words for now:

My career contributes toward bettering _____ ,

I am helping solve _____ or,

I am changing _____ .

Or, you may have a personal mission statement in either form of the following:

"I help/achieve/protect/initiate (what you do) _____ by (how you do it) _____ because (why you do it) _____ ."

Or

"I will (what you will accomplish) _____ by (when)

(e.g., I will end homelessness in my lifetime)

_____

_____ ."

Writing down your personal mission in any form will establish a solid "future anchor" for you that will provide the motivation needed to get you through the gritty parts and set you in the right direction.

Step 2: Unique You

Fill in your top three to five *values* (see Chapter 3, "Your Capabilities").

```
┌─────────────────────────────────────────────────┐
│                                                 │
│                                                 │
│                                                 │
│                                                 │
└─────────────────────────────────────────────────┘
```

Describe your unique capabilities in an "elevator pitch"—these are your "advantages" that you want to lean into (see Chapter 3, "Your Capabilities").

```
┌─────────────────────────────────────────────────┐
│                                                 │
│                                                 │
│                                                 │
└─────────────────────────────────────────────────┘
```

Keep in mind your saboteurs (see Chapter 7, "Your Conflict"), and watch out for them when they surface. Write one or two down so you are aware when it/they appear(s).

```
┌─────────────────────────────────────────────┐
│                                             │
│                                             │
│                                             │
│                                             │
└─────────────────────────────────────────────┘
```

Step 3: Timeline

First, choose a time frame for your commitment plan that will help you envision your aspirations. Consider a period between two and 10 years, depending on what feels most appropriate for you. Remember, there's no single correct answer, and you can always adjust your timeline later. The purpose of selecting a time horizon is to provide a framework for your reflections and help you articulate what you hope to achieve and experience within that specific period.

```
┌─────────────────────────────────────────────┐
│                                             │
│                                             │
│                                             │
└─────────────────────────────────────────────┘
```

Step 4: Intention

At the end of each chapter, you have already answered a deeper question that is leading you toward becoming a Well-Rewarded Disruptor—your Big Movers. These are the bold steps you want to take to move yourself forward. Here, we will draw upon those answers, and tweak them to fit in the timeline you outlined in step 3. Review your workbook summary from each chapter and draw upon those reflections to fill in your Big Movers.

Making the Big Movers tangible and conscious is incredibly powerful and transformative. They allow you to experience rapid growth. Pushing yourself also helps build confidence and resilience, especially when you come out stronger on the other side. Also, just like your personal mission, it can help you attract opportunities and the right support from others. However, for me, the most valuable part is having a sense of direction making it easier to stay aligned with my values, make tough decisions, and find fulfillment in my journey.

Next, prioritize your Big Movers. This is where you turn your motivation into a discipline. Look at your six answers and add a 1, 2, or 3 below to prioritize them for you for where you are standing today. There can be multiples of each number, and you don't have to use all the numbers (it is not a ranking exercise).

1 = It's a must on your list and you are ready to jump in

2 = It's notably important, but it can wait for the next quarter

3 = It will move the needle toward your personal mission, but other things need to happen first

	Big Mover	Priority
Capabilities		
Contribution		
Compensation		
Connection		
Conflict		
Challenge		

Step 5: Experiments in Action

Each quarter, you will pick one to three of these Big Movers to deliberately move forward. The Big Movers are usually not a single step—but a great leap that may take several years. So here we need to break them down into something you can reach in the next quarter—which we will call Experiments in Action. They are directly supporting the Big Movers you have prioritized, especially anything you have given a 1. Sometimes less results in more. It's okay to just pick one Experiment in Action per quarter—especially if you want the bulk of your energy to go toward it.

Q1/Q2/Q3/Q4, 20_ _	Experiment in Action 1	Experiment in Action 2	Experiment in Action 3
Name the experiment you are choosing.			
Let's Go! Something you will *do* to achieve this. (Action!)			
Let Go! What will you stop doing or release to clear the path forward? (Think: old habits, limiting beliefs, saboteurs)			

For each experiment (between one to three per calendar quarter), you will determine something you will *do* to move you closer toward your personal mission. You will also think of something you will need to *stop* doing or change in order to make the experiment work best. These result in actions.

Although there are always day-to-day distractions and busywork of life that features daily, your Big Movers are the signposts you are heading toward. As you say *yes* or *no* to different things, see if it aligns with your Big Mover for the quarter. We call them experiments because you won't know the outcome beforehand.

To make progress, your Experiment in Action does not necessarily have to succeed. Even if you are not successful with a specific experiment, what *did not work* is also valuable for growth. Next, in three months, we will capture the learning to make sure we remember the lessons learned from each experiment. Add an event to your calendar now for your reflection.

As a creative person, I like room for flexibility, and as long as I have my big-picture priorities clear, I make day-to-day decisions that support those priorities naturally. If you are someone who prefers more structure, you can add in an extra layer of micro-experiments weekly called SMART Goals (Specific, Measurable, Achievable, Relevant, and Time-Bound). These would outline a specific task you want to accomplish each week (or even each day) to hold you accountable to the Experiments in Action and Big Movers. Do what works best for you.

Step 6: Reflection
After three months, it's time to check in. Each quarter, you will review your experiments.

Q1/Q2/Q3/Q4, 20_ _	Experiment in Action 1	Experiment in Action 2	Experiment in Action 3
What was the experiment?			
Can you celebrate any forward progress or learning here (your growth)?			
What worked well, and why?			
What did not work, and why?			
Biggest takeaway?			

Keep your notes of all that you have accomplished each quarter. You can draw upon them to see your progress highlighting your results, which will fuel your motivation.

Take the time to celebrate your wins.

Now: revise, repeat, and record. Each quarter revisit your steps 1–4 to make sure you are still aligned before assigning your new Experiments in Action. Adjust for any changes and take the time to reflect on what you would like to move forward for next quarter.

After the reflection, design the next quarter's Experiments in Action, and repeat. This may mean focusing on the same Big Mover, but the actual experiment is different in some way based on your learning from last quarter. Finally, don't try to keep it all in your head; record your results so you can learn from them. In the workbook, there is a page you can print out or fill in online each quarter.

Harnessing all your learning from the 7 Cs and then turning your Big Movers into Experiments in Action will keep you moving forward. By taking deliberate action, within three months, you will already be able to see three months of progress. After a year, you'll be able to see a real shift. And doing the work consistently will pay off and keep the momentum going. It's more helpful to take continuous action versus occasional leaps. Opportunities in life are abundant, but they don't mean anything if you don't *start*—and then *act*.

Having all this recorded on one sheet of paper helps keep the information at your fingertips. It gives you the chance to check in easily on all these fronts and to be aware when something needs to be tweaked. It is a working document that you can keep refining as you build your ambitious career.

Your Pathway to Action

It's possible that once you get in touch with your talents and interests, your pathway will point you in the direction of the road less traveled. Maybe, as it was in the case with Kristy Drutman, it will point you in the direction where the road actually needs to be built. Taking action to build it yourself may be the only way to get where you want to go.[2]

Popularly known as "@browngirl_green" on Instagram, the 28-year-old cofounder of the Green Jobs Board (@greenjobsboard) and member of the leadership council of The Intersectional Environmentalist platform is a noted speaker, consultant, media producer, and environmental educator passionate about working at the intersections between media, diversity, and environmentalism.

The daughter of a Filipino immigrant family, when she got into UC Berkeley in 2013, Kristy was intent on studying environmental policy and becoming an environmental lawyer. She quickly got deeply involved with antifracking activism, trying to get fracking banned in the state of California. Seemingly overnight, she became a "fresh new face in California climate activism." As often as she could be found attending classes, she could be found speaking to thousands of people at rallies and other events around the country. "I was kind of like a spokesperson for being a young person who cares about the environment," she says. "And I got pretty enthralled in all of that."

At the same time, that freshman year she got hit with a lot of reality checks. "I come from an immigrant family," she says, "and my mom was helping me pay for school. And she was like, 'Why are you skipping class? Why are you doing all these things?' And that was an extra layer of pressure. I cared about people. I knew I wanted to make a difference. But at the same time, activism wasn't going to pay my bills, and my mom was making all these sacrifices for me to go to school. And that felt kind of disrespectful. You know?

"Then I remember my freshman-year roommate was a prelaw major. When I told her I wanted to become an environmental lawyer, she was like, 'Good luck with that. You're not going to make any money in that.' So I had all this anxiety already, my freshman year of college. Did I choose to study the wrong thing? No one in my family did work in this space. There's not a clear career pathway. What was I doing?"

By the end of her sophomore year, Kristy felt burned out and had fallen into what she calls an "existential crisis." Desperate to find some sort of viable avenue for putting her time and energies into making environmental and social change happen, she took a summer internship in Washington, DC, working for the Department of Housing and Urban Development. But governmental services felt distant and totally disconnected from the actual communities they served, and she knew that wasn't the right path for her passions either.

During that dislocated summer, Kristy, hungry for realness and connection, started a search for people and spaces that were talking about climate change—storytelling venues that felt alive and real, media spaces, online activism, and online advocacy groups that were connecting people through digital organization. "There weren't that many outlets," she says. "I kept asking professors and mentors and just kept telling people 'I want to do something related to media and journalism and environmentalism.' I had an intuition that that was going to matter, and everyone just thought I was crazy.

"I didn't see anyone who looked like me," she went on. "So, I was like, well, I'm going to have to figure this out and change that. I'm going to have to build my own career because the career that I was looking for just didn't exist. So I decided, 'I'm just gonna explore storytelling journalism and see what happens.'" Kristy committed through action. She created a group called the Students of Color Environmental Collective at Berkeley. In the last semester of her senior year, she decided to start her podcast, *Brown Girl Green.*

"I just started my own podcast, and it started building an audience, and people just got really into it, and I kind of just kept getting this inkling. I was like, I think this is something that I could turn into something."

One thing led to another. Creating the online Green Jobs Board for people looking for environmentally oriented jobs was one of the most logical steps for her because nothing like that existed and she passionately wished it did. "I was really frustrated about the lack of pathways. And I was like, you know what? I'm not gonna wait around for someone to create this. I'm just gonna do it. And so that's what we did."

Three years after graduation, she was invited to teach a class called "Social Media and Social Change" at the business school at UC Berkeley during the pandemic. "Ironically, I ended up in the business world, even though it was all self-taught and that wasn't what I studied," she says, laughing. "And I loved it. Basically, my whole life started evolving into this intersection of social media, journalism, online education, advocacy, and business. And it just started merging, merging, merging, to where it became my full-time job."

Instead of waiting for someone else to offer her a job or—even worse—languishing through a career where she would feel lost or undervalued, Kristy took action. She created her own ecosystem for change and committed to pursuing her contribution however she could make it work. Her action, in turn, opened opportunities for others whose own desired contributions were in line with or adjacent to hers, compounding the effect of all their efforts.

From Kristy's story, what stands out is the power of being clear and committed to a personal mission—such as bringing awareness to the urgent environmental needs of our planet. It's impressive and magnetic. Also, she intentionally took the time to understand her capabilities, and she leaned into her unique gifts. She was brave enough to notice that she needed to create her own pathway and build connections along the way to support her and uplift her. And she is a champion of continuously taking action. All this clarity helps her stand out among her peers and has allowed her to build significant momentum around her work. She will tell you her career path is not without challenges, but she feels inspired and fulfilled and is experiencing the benefits of being a Disruptor for Good.

LOOKING INWARD TO LOOK AHEAD

YOU'RE PROBABLY WONDERING HOW GRACE is doing. Thinking about the big picture of how she wanted to create a career that is *worth it* was a game changer for her. After college, she raced into a job where she clocked over 60-hour workweeks, rising in the ranks, learning a significant amount, and building her network—but all without carefully considered intention. Although she knew she was positively impacting the world, it was not *her* impact; it didn't combine the best of her capabilities or move her closer to her desired contribution. Pausing the hamster wheel of career success on someone else's terms is hard to do, but her body was watching her push herself out of alignment and was giving her all the signs that something needed adjusting.

Right before she was tempted to join a job in the Uninspired Achiever quadrant—a traditional bank—we began working together. My role is never to advise my clients but rather to ask them the right questions so that they can uncover what is truly best for them. Banking may have been the right step for her at this stage, but we needed to explore it. To get a better sense of what she wanted in her next career move, she worked through each of the 7 Cs. She had done the Myers-Briggs Assessment for a team-building experience, so she had some exposure to her capabilities, but she had never thought about the other aspects of the value she brings to the world.

She became clear on all those things and felt empowered by her uniqueness. When we initiated our work, she felt confident about her contribution. However, when digging deeper, she realized that she needed to spend the time personalizing *her* unique contribution, not just any contribution. Working on compensation was more apparent to her than the first two. She had become clear about what she needed financially and managed to let go of her own limiting beliefs about self-sacrifice. Knowing she wanted more financial compensation helped her target her search.

Connection surprised her; she had never considered her network in terms of a safety net or trampoline. And it was clear to her that she needed to learn to ask for help in both categories and yet feel confident that she was a giver at heart, so she was always going to replenish her network.

For Grace, the most important part of the work surrounding conflict was bringing forward her main saboteur: realizing that she was hyperachieving, and that was limiting her endurance. She began to see the importance of letting go of what she did not need to "hold" and working smart—not hard per se. She also was excited to learn and practice nonviolent communications skills, and she enrolled in a weekend workshop to get a head start.

The challenge was less relevant for her at this stage, because she was still experimenting with her personal mission, but having the nudge to think big was not imprinted in her mind. As such, an organized and ambitious person, having a plan in the commitment phase felt like a relief for Grace. She learned so much about herself doing all the necessary work and then getting everything on one page. Fortunately, discipline is easy for her, so she immediately set up a recurring quarterly meeting to revise and review her commitment plan—from revisiting her personal mission and values to assigning her Experiments in Action.

Doing all this work took time from her already busy schedule, but it also alleviated her stress about finding the right next move. The inquiry structure was helpful, and she was gaining a much deeper sense of awareness. Four months after we began our work, she helped create her ideal next job that happened because one of her mentors introduced her to a new contact; they hit it off immediately. For the first time, she had deep clarity about what she wanted to experience and contribute at work, and she could communicate that to others, resulting in her casting an impressive first impression on her new acquaintance. The timing was right, and she was able to suggest her ideal role that was aligned with what she wanted next, and she demonstrated how that would be beneficial for her new contact too. What's unusual is that given the circumstances, she was not competing with anyone for this role. It was hers for the making and taking. It involved working for an established organization in New York; however, she pitched starting a separate business unit that offered financial services to the types of medical organizations she had already built in her network and work she knew they needed. This brought her the financial stability she desired but also allowed her to take some business risks by building a new service with its own profit and loss responsibility in a safe environment. Furthermore, she was able to share in the financial upside of her success. She was able to hire two junior team members for her project within the first year, and she was excited to delve into managing employees too. With the consulting fees, she was able to negotiate a competitive salary that ended up giving her almost 80% more income, including her end-of-year bonus, with more upside to come in the following years (albeit the cost of living in New York was slightly higher than in Seattle). The balance of risk worked well for Grace, and of course, there is always some luck regarding timing. She is now well on her way to building a career that's *worth it*.

Your Payoff

By now you know that you don't *find* a purpose. You actively *build* one through ongoing discovery and self-reflection. If you invest in yourself, your journey will lead you to becoming the Well-Rewarded Disruptor. From watching clients work through these chapters and completing the exercises, I have witnessed them grow and benefit in four specific ways—which can even be tangible in the first three months of action (although the benefits build exponentially over time).

INTENTION

The first is intention. Intention is the foundation of building a meaningful career, and having clarity makes life less complicated. Being settled in the driver's seat of your career, directing your efforts toward your personal mission, and being deliberate with your time, is empowering. Your decisions are informed, and with this clarity, you are focused and aligned. You feel confident to forge your pathway, you know what shoulders to stand upon, and you are tuned into the rewards you receive for your work. You get to work smart, not necessarily hard.

INTEGRITY

Next is integrity. The combination of integrity with yourself and the outside world creates a powerful synergy. This alignment between your inner and outer worlds not only enhances your impact but also provides a deep sense of inner peace and satisfaction, knowing that you are being true to yourself while making a positive difference in the world.

When you have integrity with yourself, you honor your unique identity, values, and ideas, staying true to who you are and the work you are here to contribute to the world. This self-integrity requires deep self-awareness, authenticity, and the courage to embrace your individuality. You create a sense of harmony and fulfillment, knowing that you are living and working in a way that is genuine and meaningful to you.

Simultaneously, acting with integrity in your professional life means upholding your principles, commitments, and ethical standards in all your interactions and decisions. This unwavering commitment to doing what is right builds trust, credibility, and respect among colleagues, clients, and stakeholders. When you demonstrate integrity, you create a positive reputation that attracts like-minded individuals and opportunities aligned with your values.

IMPACT

Then we have impact. Your day-to-day work matters. Through self-reflection and alignment, you will naturally be on your path to impact. Combining your capabilities with your contribution will supercharge your talents, skills, and passions toward a meaningful personal mission that resonates deeply with you. As Grace realized, personalizing your unique contribution allows you to leverage your strengths and make a difference in a way that is truly fulfilling. By prioritizing impact, you leave a lasting legacy and contribute to something greater than yourself, inspiring others and creating ripple effects of positive change. It will no doubt be a career that you can be proud of.

INVINCIBILITY

Finally, we discover a feeling of being invincible. It is the inner strength and resilience you develop when building a meaningful career. When you are aligned, you have the confidence and courage to face obstacles head-on, as well as rise to the challenge when opportunities present themselves. This invincibility comes from knowing that you are doing work that matters to you and that you have the skills, network, and resources to overcome obstacles. Plus, you can turn challenges into opportunities for learning and growth, and you have the mental and emotional fortitude to persevere through setbacks and failures. This inner strength allows you to take bold risks, seize opportunities, and create the career and life you desire. You can handle the hurdles and are driven to push past the hard work for the outcome you dream about.

As you may have noticed, these four benefits all start with *I*. That is deliberate because the necessary work is within you first and foremost. You are at the center of your potential.

Stamina

Ninety thousand hours is a long time. It's well beyond a marathon; it's a lifelong trek. And if you are someone dedicated to making the world a better place, we really need you and your contribution in the game for as long as possible. But without some rest and some fun, it's not sustainable.

I would like you to consider dividing your day into three buckets. In each day you either are working, playing, or recharging. Notice which bucket you are attending to, and make sure they are all given attention. You'll intuitively know when you are feeling great and finding the right balance between the three. If you find yourself out of balance, assess what you might shift, and make the change.

Figure 10.1. Working, Recharging, and Playing Buckets

We all measure these differently. For some people, physical exercise feels like work. For others, it's an amazing recharge. Or it's their play. Just make sure you are tapping into all three buckets each week. There is no prize for overworking. To get to your personal mission, you will need to figure out how to do things differently so that you can go the distance. Of course, discovering your personal mission and prioritizing it is a huge head start. But if you're on the fast track, be mindful about taking care of yourself. Each one of us needs to take responsibility for creating the kind of balance in our lives that will enable us to stay the course.

In addition, to stay healthy, you need to take care of yourself. Nourish your body with real food. Prioritize your sleep by establishing healthy sleep habits, such as a regular sleep schedule. Manage stress—and become aware of your stress levels. This might include practices like meditation, mindfulness, deep breathing exercises, and activities that promote relaxation and rejuvenation.

Incorporate regular physical activities in your schedule to keep your body moving. Movement is life and crucial for maintaining optimal health and vitality. Finally, cultivate emotional well-being through positive relationships, expressing gratitude, engaging in mindfulness or therapy, laughing, and finding joy in everyday life. None of these activities will provide the balance you need on their own, but combined with an intentional approach to your life and work, they can make the process more sustainable.

Finding Your Way

Early on in your career journey lies an important window to experiment with ideas and jobs to find the things that light you up. It could be by pursuing anything that surfaced while reading the previous chapters. But also experiment on how to land all your magic in a paid working environment. Try out a larger well-established company, or a small start-up, or imagine yourself as a solopreneur (examples of all of these appear throughout the book). Only once you have an idea of what is exciting, and worth your hours, it is time to deepen your expertise. Why? Because as life transpires, you are likely to increase your responsibilities (for example, you may choose to invest in a house or start a family), which then changes your risk profile. Unless you want to wait until retirement, your best opportunity is now.

I have had so many conversations with people later in their career where they share that they have been "climbing the wrong ladder," or "chasing a version of success that they no longer subscribe to," only to find that they are not doing what's important to them. These are conversations of regret. Why does that happen? One common reason is that they jumped straight onto the "career hamster wheel," racing for "the top." With only two weeks of paid vacation a year as the standard in the US, there is barely any time to gain perspective, resulting in feeling stuck or on autopilot, rather than working toward your fulfillment.

Trying out different opportunities does not mean you have to change jobs frequently, although that's not off the table for the right reasons. Alternatively, within some companies you can do projects outside of your department too, to gain further insights and develop relationships beyond your group. Other ways to experiment include internships, micro-internships, apprenticeships, rotating management programs, consulting on the side, attending conferences, or volunteering on the weekends. Even listening to TED Talks, reading books, or watching documentaries can help you find your path. All these ideas will expose you to lots of different roles, environments, and things you may care deeply about and want to explore.

Your Individual Efforts Will Count

Holding on to hope is something that humans are exceptionally good at. As you contribute toward the issues that are most relevant to you, remember that meaningful change is rarely instantaneous. However, history shows us that committed individuals coming together can reshape society against the odds. Hope can keep you motivated in the meantime.

For us to see change happen sooner rather than later, we don't need 100% of the population to believe in climate change, the need for equal pay for women, or equal rights of underrepresented groups across the world. Let me explain. Compelling research by political scientist Erica Chenoweth has found that nonviolent civil disobedience is the most powerful way to shape world politics.[1] Analyzing hundreds of campaigns over the last century, Chenoweth discovered that nonviolent campaigns are twice as likely to achieve their goals compared to violent campaigns. Notably, her work demonstrates that it takes around 3.5% of the population actively participating in peaceful protests to create serious political change. Now your career may not include physical peaceful protests with signs and demonstrations—but through your work, you may find you are doing the same thing, in a different form, and that seems achievable.

Other studies corroborate the idea that minority views can wield outsized influence and catalyze social tipping points. Research from the University of Pennsylvania and the University of London suggests that when just 25% of people hold a minority opinion, they can successfully sway the majority and overturn conventional thinking. At that critical mass, contrarians in online experiments were able to convert 72%–100% of their groups to adopt a new position.[2]

I want you to know that your work counts and can make a real difference. From evolving attitudes around gender, race, and social justice, to issues like drug policy reform, societal transformations often start with impassioned people like you who courageously challenge or disrupt the status quo. As the researchers in the previous study note, "approaching that tipping point is slow going, and you can see backsliding. But once you get over it, you'll see a really large-scale impact."

Remember, you are part of an interconnected ecosystem of changemakers, so you are not doing this alone. Others with similar values and interests are equally devoted to progress, and your collective power grows exponentially. Alongside them, you can reach that critical tipping point.

Tuning in to Your Inner Rebel

"It is difficult to get a man to understand something when his salary depends on his not understanding it," wrote the author Upton Sinclair.[3] You may have noticed the deliberate use of the word "disruptor" in the Good for You, Good for the World framework. It certainly is backward that wanting to look after the planet, and its wildlife, including humans, makes you a disruptor, a rebel, or an activist. It does not make sense to me why we still need to highlight a company's social impact standing versus requiring the companies that are low impact, or negative impactors to be labeled, transparent, and accountable. Simply put, in accumulation, our work either hurts the world or helps the world. Yet we are only caretakers here on Earth and our planet is not ours to destroy. You and I are here because we *know* we need to change things up, and fast— which only a disruptor can do.

> It certainly is backward that wanting to look after the planet, and its wildlife, including humans, makes you a disruptor, a rebel, or an activist.

If you can answer yes to these two important questions, then you are a disruptor in today's world.

- Is your career good for you?

and

- Is it good for the world?

What's Next for You?

By now you know my general views and wishes for how to build a career that motivates you. Through coaching training, I learned early on that I cannot want something for you more than you want it for yourself. I am hopeful that we are aligned, and that you are excited to make your noteworthy contribution. In any coaching program, closing the session is as important and meaningful as the start. Capturing your learning and reflecting on what will change in your life from today is worth considering. You are worthy of a career that ignites your spirit and broadens your heart. I'm optimistic about this upcoming generation of young adults. I also know that finding your path can be frustrating and challenging. I have created several additional options to further help you along your way.

First, wherever you have landed, I would love to hear from you. Send us your personal mission statement when it's ready to info@georgienthoven.com, and we will share it with our community of disruptors.

Next, I have a free podcast also called *Work That's Worth It* (which you can find on Apple, Spotify, or anywhere you get your podcasts) where I interview people I admire highlighting their career pathways and how they became disruptors for good. I aim to make it super easy for you to broaden your options and get a feel for different roles and industries—perhaps helping set you off in a meaningful direction. I hope you will tune in to the episodes that spark your interest. And feel free to share it with your like-minded friends.

Third, if you need help processing and organizing the information that you have surfaced in the workbook, or more community support, please visit the Resources page for this book at www.workthatsworthit.com/resources.

Lastly, stay tuned by following me on social media on Instagram and Facebook at @georgienthoven.

As you proceed on your ambitious career journey, keep asking yourself: What is the problem I am solving? And then: Is this problem worth my time and energy? I am confident your answers to these questions will guide you in the right direction: onward.

AFTERWORD

WRITING THIS BOOK HAS INVOLVED so much more than putting my thoughts into words, and I am so excited that you have chosen to read it. If the insights shared in this book—drawn from my experiences, the inspiring journeys of my clients, and the wisdom of experts—serve as a catalyst for the positive impact you create and ignite in the world, then I will feel profoundly grateful.

Having never written a book before or built a personal brand platform, with the big picture in mind, I took each step one at a time, continually moving forward, and the right doors have graciously opened at just the right moments.

As Vincent Stanley, an employee for more than 50 years at Patagonia, said to me, "Know what moves you and what satisfies you, because work is 90% chores."[1] Excitement for the authentic contribution I could create fueled my motivation to sit down and do the work of researching, organizing, and writing. Because I have true clarity regarding my calling, for the first time in my career, I have experienced a flow state where I work long hours but the work itself refuels me, letting me experience the

Upward Spiral. This doesn't mean it hasn't taken a *lot* of intellectual bravery and a lot of emotional hard work to build up my self-confidence, design the framework, test it on clients, and then face the start of every chapter. However, I am notably energized despite these challenges.

Approaching ambitious and successful people (my role models!) to interview for the book felt intimidating at first. But I was met again and again with open arms, and generously offered their shoulders to stand upon. Everyone could relate to the topic from some angle. My closest friends and family offered me ideas and support and did not let me give up. People I had not talked to in years made time to share their stories and introduce me to their networks. Even blind contacts said yes and were eager to contribute and share their very personal journeys with me and now you.

This felt surprising at first. But it reminded me that when you are doing good, doors open easily. As Margaret Renkl, a *New York Times* opinion writer, recently shared in her graduation speech to the students of Sewanee, University of the South: "If you remember only two things: The world is beautiful. People are good."[2] At the very least, there is beauty in the world and beauty in every human. Focusing on bringing out the beauty in each becomes contagious.

All the same, this project has pushed me well beyond what is comfortable and familiar, and propelled me deep into my expansion zone. It has required me to be more vulnerable than ever before, to trust the universe, and to draw upon my motivation and discipline, and every tool in my toolkit to stay on course. I am 100% a better person for having done it. And I feel proud to have been able to show my kids—who have witnessed me working all hours of the day and night over this past year—how to trust yourself and bring to life your important and unique contribution.

———

A final note—and a request for a kind act.

If this book has helped you in any way, whether big or small, you have an opportunity to pay it forward (and back) with a simple act of kindness. By writing a review, you can help spread the message of *Work That's Worth It* by inspiring others to join our collective mission of taking care of each other and our planet.

In today's digital world, algorithms used by platforms like Amazon and Goodreads play a crucial role in determining a book's visibility and reach. Your honest review, no matter how brief, can make a significant difference in helping this book's message find its way to more readers who are eager to make a positive impact.

If you found value in these pages, please take a moment to share your thoughts and leave a review. Your support not only means a great deal to me personally, but it also contributes to the larger movement of people dedicating their time and talents to creating a better world for all.

Thank you in advance for your kindness and for being a part of this journey toward a more compassionate, sustainable future. Together, we can create ripples of positive change that will extend far beyond our own lives.

ACKNOWLEDGMENTS

THIS BOOK, MUCH LIKE THE meaningful work it advocates for, is the result of countless conversations, collaborations, and moments of inspiration. I'm profoundly grateful to everyone who supported and contributed to my efforts in bringing to the world my first book: *Work That's Worth It.*

To my beautiful family: You are at the foundation of everything that I care for. Roberto, Sienna, Oliver, and Patrick—thank you for indulging me in this creative process, even when it took time and focus from all of you. Roberto, it's no surprise that you have been my biggest supporter in this endeavor; you are the kindest person I know, and your encouragement allowed me to push through moments of vulnerability and doubt. Sienna, your natural tendency to lead with compassion motivated me to explore interesting role models who may excite you as you determine your life path and future contribution. You are the queen of making things happen. Oliver, your extraordinary sense of justice and ability to form deep relationships inspire me to make worthy choices and take on this challenge worth my time. And Patrick, you were born remarkably aware and aligned with the natural world, wisely seeing where adults are making poor decisions. Your clarity is my wake-up call and my constant source of commitment to this work. You all stayed interested, asking me questions, giving me marketing ideas, and offering unwavering support. You have inspired this creative adventure to contribute my part to our beautiful planet and become a Disruptor for Good in my own right.

To my (mostly) girl squad—my inner circle—thank you for your endless encouragement, coaching, door-opening, listening, boundary support, and accountability. Including my business squad: thank you for the behind-the-scenes logo design, website building, and social media help. And for keeping me connected to my heart (and less in my head) through amazing coaching and therapy. You've all been integral to my own Upward Spiral, pushing me to enhance my capabilities and expand my connections. I am grateful for the books and articles you shared, the details we chewed on, the people you introduced me to, for not letting me give up when faced with challenges, and for the much-needed laughs when I needed a distraction. In particular, my fellow mothers, our careers are often not linear, and we need to lean into supporting each other to keep expressing our creative experiments at all stages of life. We have the runway to keep exploring and contributing at any age. And a reminder for those who need it: you don't need permission to contribute positively to this world; you just need to care. Count on me for your endeavors down the road.

To my editor, Nathan True, your transparency, insights, and guidance were invaluable in redirecting some messy thoughts and shaping them into the book's best form. To Greenleaf, thank you for saying yes to being my publisher, for waiting patiently to get my words together, for professionalizing my work, and showing me how the book world works. Working with newbies must be challenging, and I am grateful for your niche, helping authors on a mission, like me. To Brand Builders Group, narrowing in on Grace is thanks to you.

To my trampoline team, I'm indebted to the many inspiring role models who gracefully told me about their career journeys. Sharing your stories allows me to bounce higher: thank you Vincent Stanley, Sami Inkinen, Debbie Sterling, Ntefeleng Nene, Jessica Lindl, Amy King, Bernard Law, Jeremy Schifeling, and Kristy Drutman. Your experiences bring the concepts in this book to life and provide examples of the pathways to get there, showcasing how to navigate conflict, embrace challenges, and maintain an unwavering commitment to meaningful work. I thoroughly enjoyed every conversation we had, and connecting with you is part of my reward. It was extraordinary to discover how similar you all are in what you value and prioritize (albeit different personal missions), and to understand of your roles as Disruptors for Good. Your shared perspectives and unique journeys have been instrumental in shaping the core ideas of this work.

Thank you to the young professionals who have trusted me to guide them to discover their chosen career paths through coaching. Working with you, and listening to your ideas and experiences, helped me know what questions we needed to answer in this book. Your work matters, and I can't wait to see where your ambition takes you. Keep making sure you tune into the rewards for your valuable work too.

My most vulnerable thank-yous go to the first set of beta readers who sent me back to the drawing board to better define my target audience and message—you pushed me to look inward to look ahead. And to my second round of readers, one of whom shared that she "had already reached out to one of the companies in the book" after feeling inspired. I view honest feedback as a generous gift—and my book owes you all! Your perspectives enhanced this work immeasurably and helped shape it into a true guide for those seeking to make the most of their 90,000-hour career.

To you, the reader—thank you for picking up this book as you build your Work That's Worth It. My hope is that these pages inspire and guide you on your journey to becoming a Well-Rewarded Disruptor, helping you stay aligned with your gifts to create your own powerful Upward Spiral.

Beyond humans, thank you, beautiful San Francisco Bay, for greeting me with your beauty on my daily hikes through the woods and coastline. Nature kept me balanced and replenished with its beauty, helping me settle my mind and fuel my creative spark (and recalibrate my laptop posture too!). And to Portugal for your creative portals and planting the seed for my calling.

Lastly, just to shout from the rooftops: it's so hard to step into vulnerability. If you have people in your life taking chances, support them. The world is better with more authentic voices.

NOTES

Introduction

1. Julianne McShane, "Most Americans Just Aren't into Their Jobs, New Gallup Data Shows," NBC News, January 26, 2023, https://www.nbcnews .com/business/business-news/americans-just-arent-jobs-new-gallup-data -shows-rcna67653. See also, "Gen Z Workforce: Values as the Catalyst for Job Change," *LinkedIn Pulse* (blog), June 1, 2023, https://www .linkedin.com/pulse/gen-z-workforce-values-catalyst-job-change-inop-ai/. See also, New Standard Institute, "94% of Generation Z Consumers Believe Companies Have a Responsibility to Address Environmental and Social Issues," The Information – New Standard Institute, https://www .newstandardinstitute.org/the-information/94-of-generation-z-consumers -believe-companies-have-a-responsibility-to-address-environmental-and -social-issues53 (accessed September 10, 2024).

2. Boris Thurm, Sophie Bürgin, and Jordan Widner, "Let's Replace GDP: Introducing the Green Domestic Product," IMD, September 21, 2022, https://www.imd.org/ibyimd/sustainability/lets-replace-gdp-introducing -the-green-domestic-product. See also, Tejvan Pettinger, "Genuine Progress Indicator GPI v. GDP," *Economics Help* (blog), February 22, 2011, https:// www.economicshelp.org/blog/2666/economics/genuine-progress-indicator -gpi-v-gdp. See also, Hot or Cool – Happy Planet Index, "How Happy Is the Planet?," https://happyplanetindex.org (accessed September 10, 2024).

3. B Lab Global, "B Lab Global Site." Accessed December 2024. https://www .bcorporation.net/en-us/.

4. Susan Peppercorn, "Why You Should Stop Trying to Be Happy at Work," *Harvard Business Review*, July 26, 2019, https://hbr.org/2019/07/why-you -should-stop-trying-to-be-happy-at-work.

5. Victoria Sansone, "Responsible Business Lessons from Patagonia," Wharton Stories – The Wharton School of Business at The University of Pennsylvania, February 12, 2020, https://www.wharton.upenn.edu/story /responsible-business-lessons-from-patagonia. See also, Interview with Vincent Stanley, January 7, 2023.

Chapter 2

1. Interview with Sami Inkinen, January 6, 2023.

2. American Diabetes Association, "Fast Facts: Data and Statistics about Diabetes," January 2022, https://professional.diabetes.org/sites/default/files /media/diabetes_fast_facts22322.pdf.

3. Emily D. Parker et al., "Economic Costs of Diabetes in the U.S. in 2017," *Diabetes Care* 41, no. 5 (2018): 917–928.

4. Sami Inkinen, "When Profits Fuel Purpose Magic Happens," *Sami Inkinen* (blog), January 7, 2024, https://www.samiinkinen.com/post/155562616337 /when-profits-fuel-purpose-magic-happens.

5. S. J. Hallberg et al., "Effectiveness and Safety of a Novel Care Model for the Management of Type 2 Diabetes at One Year: An Open Label, Non-Randomized, Controlled Study," Diabetes Therapy 9, no. 2 (2018): 583–612.

6. A. L. McKenzie et al., "Type 2 Diabetes Prevention Focused on Normalization of Glycemia: A Two-Year Pilot Study," *Nutrients* 13, no. 3 (2021): 749.

7. Hallberg et al., "Effectiveness and Safety of a Novel Care Model." See also, "Type 2 Diabetes," Virta Health, https://www.virtahealth.com /type2diabetes#reversing-type-2 (accessed September 13, 2024).

8. "Greta Thunberg: Who Is the Climate Activist and What Has She Achieved?," BBC News, May 9, 2024, https://www.bbc.com/news/world -europe-49918719.

9. See the Jane Goodall Institute's website at www.janegoodall.org (accessed September 10, 2024). See also, Henry Nicholls, "Jane Goodall: How She Redefined Mankind," BBC, March 31, 2014, https://www.bbc.com/future /article/20140331-the-woman-who-redefined-mankind.

10. Lou Adler, "New Survey Reveals 85% of All Jobs Are Filled via Networking," *LinkedIn Pulse* (blog), February 29, 2016, https://www .linkedin.com/pulse/new-survey-reveals-85-all-jobs-filled-via-networking -lou-adler.

11. Amanda Augustine, "4 Trends Job Seekers Can Expect in 2024 That Will Impact Their Search," *Fast Company*, December 27, 2023, https://www .fastcompany.com/90996990/trends-jobseekers-2024-impact-search.

Chapter 3

1. Eva M. Krockow, "How Many Decisions Do We Make Each Day?," *Psychology Today, Attention* (blog), September 27, 2018, https://www.psychologytoday.com/us/blog/stretching-theory/201809/how-many-decisions-do-we-make-each-day.

2. Jane Margolis and Allan Fisher, *Unlocking the Clubhouse: Women in Computing* (Cambridge, Massachusetts: MIT Press, 2002).

3. Katherine Shaver, "Female Dummy Makes Her Mark on Male-Dominated Crash Tests," *Washington Post*, March 25, 2012, https://www.washingtonpost.com/local/trafficandcommuting/female-dummy-makes-her-mark-on-male-dominated-crash-tests/2012/03/07/gIQANBLjaS_story.html.

4. Find the Values in Action (VIA) Character Survey at www.viacharacter.org (accessed September 10, 2024).

5. Find the CliftonStrengths Assessment at https://www.gallup.com/cliftonstrengths. See also, the Myers-Briggs Type Indicator Assessment at www.myersbriggs.org. See also, the Enneagram Personality Test at www.enneagraminstitute.com/store (accessed September 10, 2024).

6. Sonya Bessalel, "LinkedIn 2024 Most In-Demand Skills: Learn the Skills Companies Need Most," *LinkedIn Business Learning* (blog), February 8, 2024, https://www.linkedin.com/business/learning/blog/top-skills-and-courses/most-in-demand-skills. See also, Victoria Masterson, "Future of Jobs 2023: These Are the Most In-Demand Skills Now—and Beyond," World Economic Forum – Agenda, May 1, 2023, https://www.weforum.org/agenda/2023/05/future-of-jobs-2023-skills.

7. World Economic Forum – Publications, "The Future of Jobs Report 2023," April 30, 2023, https://www.weforum.org/publications/the-future-of-jobs-report-2023/digest.

Chapter 4

1. Melody Wilding, "Do You Have a Job, Career or Calling? The Difference Matters," *Forbes*, April 23, 2018, https://www.forbes.com/sites/melodywilding/2018/04/23/do-you-have-a-job-career-or-calling-the-difference-matters.

2. Katharine Brooks, "Job, Career, Calling: Key to Happiness and Meaning at Work?," *Psychology Today, Career* (blog), June 29, 2012, https://www.psychologytoday.com/us/blog/career-transitions/201206/job-career-calling-key-happiness-and-meaning-work.

3. Interview with Debbie Sterling, July 22, 2024.

4. World Economic Forum "Appendix B: Global Risks Perception Survey 2023–2024" in "Global Risks Report 2024," Publications – January 10, 2024, https://www.weforum.org/publications/global-risks-report-2024 /in-full/appendix-b-global-risks-perception-survey-2023-2024.

5. "About Us," Pippa Small Jewelry, https://pippasmall.com/en-us/pages/about (accessed September 10, 2024).

6. William Pickworth, "Sadio Mane Has Transformed the Lives of African Villagers with Hospital Build and School Donations," *Liverpool Echo*, June 21, 2022, https://www.liverpoolecho.co.uk/sport/football/football-news /sadio-mane-hospital-school-donations-24279775.

Chapter 5

1. Caitlin Kearney, "The Price of Doing Good: Measuring the Nonprofit Pay Cut," PayScale – Research and Insights, November 27, 2018, https://www .payscale.com/research-and-insights/nonprofit-pay-cut.

2. Caitlyn Shelton, "State-by-State Teacher Shortages (and What They're Doing about It)," NewsNation, updated January 26, 2023, https://www .newsnationnow.com/us-news/education/education-reform/hold-how -each-state-is-solving-its-teacher-shortage-and-could-you-become-a-teacher. See also, Tuan D. Nguyen, Chanh B. Lam, and Paul Bruno, "Is There a National Teacher Shortage? A Systematic Examination of Reports of Teacher Shortages in the United States," Annenberg Institute Working Paper, August 2022, https://edworkingpapers.com/ai22-631.

3. Yvon Chouinard, "Earth Is Now Our Only Shareholder," Patagonia, September 14, 2022, https://www.patagonia.com/ownership.

4. Fifth Wall, "About," Fifth Wall, https://fifthwall.com/about (accessed September 10, 2024).

5. "About Loop," Loop Global, https://loopglobal.com/about/#charging -solutions (accessed September 10, 2024).

6. "Fifth Wall Closes $500 Million for Its First Climate Fund," Business Wire, July 21, 2022, https://www.businesswire.com/news/home/20220721005373 /en/Fifth-Wall-Closes-500-Million-for-its-First-Climate-Fund.

7. See Develop for Good's website at https://www.developforgood.org (accessed August 28, 2024).

8. Interview with Ntefeleng Nene, March 16, 2023.

Chapter 6

1. Private event in San Francisco cohosted by Common Sense Media, April 2021.

2. "Invest in Your Relationship: The Emotional Bank Account," Gottman Institute, *Love & Relationships* (blog), last updated June 26, 2024, https://www.gottman.com/blog/invest-relationship-emotional-bank-account/.

3. Interview with Jessica Lindl, May 23, 2023.

4. Interview with Amy King, February 23, 2023.

5. See the Pallet website at https://docsend.com/view/cj662tr36qkkk2tw/d/imjdy97wvdrsdssx (accessed September 13, 2024).

6. Jim Rohn, quoted in *The Success Principles* by Jack Canfield with Janet Switzer (New York: HarperCollins, 2005).

7. Find the life cycle assessment (LCA) tool at https://www.allbirds.com/pages/carbon-footprint-calculator (accessed September 10, 2024).

8. Interview with Bernard Law, November 11, 2022.

Chapter 7

1. See the Center for Non-Violent Communications at https://www.cnvc.org (accessed September 10, 2024).

2. The original edition is by Roger Fisher and William Ury, *Getting to Yes: Negotiating Agreement without Giving In* (Boston: Houghton Mifflin, 1981); the latest update, in 2011, adds Bruce Patton as a coauthor.

3. P. F. Drucker, *The Frontiers of Management* (New York: Truman Talley Books, 1986).

4. Paul Coelho, *Aleph* (New York: Knopf, 2011).

5. Robin Shrum, "When It Comes to Leadership, Self-Awareness Matters. Here's Why," EducationWeek, June 5, 2023, https://www.edweek.org/leadership/opinion-when-it-comes-to-leadership-self-awareness-matters-heres-why/2023/06.

6. "How We Self-Sabotage," test, Positive Intelligence, https://www.positiveintelligence.com/saboteurs (accessed August 28, 2024).

7. Quoted at www.positiveintelligence.com/saboteurs (accessed September 10, 2024).

8. Interview with Judy Wilkins-Smith, May 2019.

Chapter 8

1. Interview with Jeremy Schifeling, March 28, 2023.

2. "What Is the History of Khan Academy?," Khan Academy, last updated 2022, https://support.khanacademy.org/hc/en-us/articles/202483180-What-is-the-history-of-Khan-Academy.

3. Joseph Lucco, "The Eisenhower Principle Applied to Business Strategy Management," *ClearPoint Strategy* (blog), August 19, 2024, https://www.clearpointstrategy.com/blog/eisenhower-principle-and-business-strategy-management.

Chapter 9

1. Sarah Ban Breathnach, *A Man's Journey to Simple Abundance* (New York: Scribner, 2000).
2. Interview with Kristy Drutman, January 5, 2023.

Conclusion

1. David Robson, "The '3.5% Rule': How a Small Minority Can Change the World," BBC, May 13, 2019, https://www.bbc.com/future/article/20190513-it-only-takes-35-of-people-to-change-the-world.
2. David Noonan, "The 25% Revolution: How Big Does a Minority Have to Be to Reshape Society?," *Scientific American*, June 8, 2018, https://www.scientificamerican.com/article/the-25-revolution-how-big-does-a-minority-have-to-be-to-reshape-society.
3. Upton Sinclair, *I, Candidate for Governor: And How I Got Licked* (Berkeley: University of California Press, [1935] 1994).

Afterword

1. Interview with Vincent Stanley, January 6, 2023.
2. Margaret Renkl, "Graduates, My Generation Wrecked So Much That's Precious. How Can I Offer You Advice?," *New York Times* – opinion, May 15, 2023, https://www.nytimes.com/2023/05/15/opinion/letter-to-graduates-hope-despair.html.

ABOUT THE AUTHOR

GEORGI ENTHOVEN IS AN INTERNATIONAL thought leader, trusted advisor, and first-time author of *Work That's Worth It*. As a visionary thought leader, Georgi specializes in unearthing the unique inspiration and career desires of her clients, guiding them on a transformative journey toward building a career that's good for them and for the world. She is an optimist at heart and has a special talent for seeing potential in others. She is a firm believer that business can be used as a force for positive change in the world, and therefore is driven to elevate kindhearted people with empathy into positions of influence and leadership.

Georgi is a distinguished alumna of the University of California at Berkeley and Harvard Business School, where she earned her master's in business administration. Her career has been anything but conventional; she often describes it as "taking the scenic route" (although the common thread throughout her career is "meaningful contribution"). Having lived in more than half a dozen countries, including South Africa, Canada, the United Kingdom, Australia,

Mexico, and the United States, she treasures a truly global perspective, including the dynamics of emerging markets.

Driven by a passion for contribution and a relentless focus on solving real-world problems, she has worked with organizations as a founder, operating in executive roles and board positions, both for-profit and not-for-profit. She plays a pivotal role in fostering and designing businesses that positively influence its customers and community. Georgi is known for her collaborative spirit and her ability to bring compassion and creativity to any endeavor. If you are seated next to her at dinner, she is likely to ask what you care about, versus what you do.

Outside her professional endeavors, Georgi places family at the forefront of her priorities. Her love for adventures, or "Adventuras," reflects her commitment to prioritize experiences over material possessions. Georgi lives in San Francisco and shares her life with her loving husband, Roberto, and three bicultural children, Sienna, Oliver, and Patrick, who bring joy and richness to her life every day.

www.ingramcontent.com/pod-product-compliance
Lightning Source LLC
Chambersburg PA
CBHW030503210326
41597CB00013B/768